THE
AFRO-AMERICAN
WORLD
ALMANAC

THE
AFRO-AMERICAN
WORLD
ALMANAC

What Do You Know About Your Race?

With Unusual Historic Facts About
Prominent People Of African Descent
From A To Z

ROSS D. BROWN

INPRINT EDITIONS

Baltimore

THE AFRO-AMERICAN WORLD ALMANAC

First published 1943
Published 1999 by
INPRINT EDITIONS

ISBN 1-58073-018-3

Cover art by Michelle D. Wright

Printed by BCP Digital Printing
An affiliate company of Black Classic Press

ABOUT INPRINT EDITIONS

Our mission is to keep good books in print. We give life to books that might never be published or republished by making them available On Demand. Manuscripts and books are scanned, stored, and then printed as single or multiple copies from our digital library. When reprinting out-of-print books, we always use the best copy available.

INPRINT EDITIONS are especially useful to scholars, students, and general readers who have an interest in enjoying all that books have to offer. Our books are also a valuable resource for libraries in search of replacement copies.

You can purchase books or obtain a curent list of our titles from:

INPRINT EDITIONS
c/o Black Classic Press
P. O. Box 13414
Baltimore, MD 21203
Also visit our website:
www.blackclassic.com

— DEDICATED —
TO THE MINISTERS, CHURCHES, INSURANCE
COMPANIES, SOCIETIES AND CLUBS
WHO HAVE SO LOYALLY AIDED
IN THE PROMOTION OF
THIS WORK.

I HAVE DUG DOWN, AND I WANT YOU TO PRESS FORWARD, DRINK DEEP, THINK HARD, AND WORK FAST.

SOMETHING TO REMEMBER

The Southern slave owners said we were "Darkies"

The Race hating crackers called us "Niggers"

The Black Brotherhood said we were "Black People"

The Moorish Americans said we were "Asiatics"

The A. M. E. Church founder called us "Africans"

The U· N. I. A. says we are "Negroes"

The N. A. A. C. P. says we are "Colored People"

The Holy Bible refers to us as "Ethiopians"

Many newspapers refer to us as a "Group"

And before election politicians call us "Brothers"

Whatever we are, we will soon pass out of existance as a race, unless we stop trying to get something for nothing.

If we fail to remember who we are, we should always remember where we are, and if the men and women of our race continue their vulgarity, profanity and indecency on the streets and in public places, if we do not cultivate a higher standard of culture, dignity and refinement, we will soon be pushed off the face of the earth.

AUTHOR

REV. ROSS D. BROWN

Founder and Pastor "Truth Seeker's Temple"
Mailing Address, 417 East 47th Street, Room 302, Chicago, Ill.

PRICE ONE DOLLAR - PLUS POSTAGE BY MAIL

If this book meets with your approval, you can help in no better way
than to pass it on to your friends

CONTENTS

AFRO-AMERICAN WORLD ALMANAC

JANUARY

1—1863—ABRAHAM LINCOLN issued Emancipation Proclamation, freeing slaves as a war measure.

2—1831—JO. ANDERSON—a slave at Steels Tavern, Va., was co-inventor of the first mechanical reaper.

3—1868—Two days previous, PERRY PARKER was born.

4—1799—GEORGE WASHINGTON owned 300 black slaves.

5—1943—GEORGE W. CARVER died Tuskegee, Ala., world's greatest Agricultural Chemist.

6—1938—SINCE 1882—Mississippi has had 595 lynchings.

7—1922—COL. CHARLES YOUNG died in Liberia, West Africa, great soldier, West Point graduate.

8—1492—PETRO ALONZO was the black navigator with Columbus when America was discovered.

9—1900—GEORGE DIXON lost featherweight title to Terry McGovern in 9 rounds, Brooklyn, N. Y.

10—1905—BRUCE FLOWERS, pugalist, born in New Rochelle, N. Y.

11—1757—ALEXANDER HAMILTON was born in West Indian Islands.

12—1890—MORDECIA W. JOHNSON, born Paris Henry Co. Tennessee, Clergyman, Educator, President Howard University.

13—1919—MACK WATSON—a U. S. Soldier in France, was cited for bravery.

14—1923—B. T. TANNER DIED—Bishop of the African Methodist Episcopal Church.

15—1881—WILLIAM PICKENS—born Anderson Co. S. C., Educator, Author.

JANUARY

16—1918—JACKIE WILSON, welterweight boxer was born in Spencer, N. C.

17—1867—J. M. LANGSTON granted privilage to practice law before U. S. Supreme Court.

18—1842—POOR AND WEALTHY NEGROES contributed to the auxiliaries of the Catholic church.

19—1788—FIRST AFRICAN BAPTIST CHURCH organized in Savannah, Ga., still in use.

20—IN 1831 NAT TURNER— The Insurrectionist killed over 60 white people before he was killed.

21—JOE GANS—Lightweight champion is buried in Auburn cemetry, Baltimore, Md.

22—1943—PAUL ROBESON, famed Negro Radio, Concert singer, canceled his engagement in Wilmington, Del., because of discrimination.

23—1849—J. M. GREGORY was born.   Business man, orator and educator.

24—1863—LESS THAN ONE TENTH of the Mulattoes were slaves.

25—1917—NEGROES HELD MASS Meeting in Richmond, Va., opposing colonizing in Liberia, Africa.

25—1942—CLEO WRIGHT was lynched in Sikeston, Missouri.

26—1922—U. S. CONGRESS passed Dyer Anti-Lynching bill.

27—1913—J. J. PLANTVIGNE died in Baltimore, Maryland, was one of few Negro Catholic Priests.

28—1865—FRED DOUGLASS was the greatest orator of his day.

29—1876—JAMES A. COBB was born, Municipal Judge Arcadia, Louisiana.

30—1875—JOHN W. ROBERTS died in Liberia. First Negro Missionary Bishop of the Methodist Episcopal Church.

31—1943—WILLIAM H. HASTIE, civilian aide to Henry L. Stimson, Secretary of War, resigned his post because of discrimination against Negroes in the air force.

FEBRUARY

1—1902—LANGSTON HUGHES — born Joplin, Mo., student and poet.
2—1895—FREDERICK DOUGLASS died, noted American, anti-slavery, agitator and statesman.
3—BENJAMINE BANNEKER — helped plan and survey Washington, D. C.
4—1794—EMANCIPATION of the Slaves of the Colonies of France.
5—1858—C. T. WALKER was born, noted minister of Augusta, Georgia.
6—1938—NEGRO CHURCH PROPERTY is worth over two hundred million dollars.
7—THE U. S. PATENT OFFICE keeps no separate record of patents by Negroes.
8—1943—JACQUELINE, a 7 pound, 5 ounce baby girl was born to Mr. and Mrs. Joe Louis, Chicago, Ill.
9—1906—PAUL LAURANCE DUNBAR died, Dayton, Ohio, America's foremost lyric poet.
10—1837—ALEXANDER S. PUSHKIN, Great Russian poet died after a duel with D'Anthens, Petersburg, Russia.
11—1896—Three days later ISAAC MURPHY died, great jockey, won three Kentucky Derbies and three American Derbies.
12—1917—JAMES D. CORROTHERS, died, great poet and preacher.
13—1873—EMMET J. SCOTT was born, educator, secretary to Booker T. Washington.
14—1760—RICHARD ALLEN was born, founded A.M.E. Church in Philadelphia, because of prejudice against his race.
15—1919—BIRMINGHAM, ALA. RIOT—Policeman and Negro killed.
16—1854—PROF. W. S. SCORBOROUGH was born, Macon Georgia, professor of classical Greek.
17—1907—PROF. W. E. B. DUBOIS spoke before Ethical Culture Society in New York City.

FEBRUARY

18—1877—JOHN A. GREGG, born Eureka, Kansas, University President and A.M.E. Church Bishop.

19—1924—WHITE STUDENTS at West Point still make it unpleasant for Negro students.

20—1876—One day later, JOSEPH JENKINS ROBERTS died, first man of color to rule Liberia. Born in Virginia, 1809.

21—1938—ANTI-LYNCHING BILL set aside after southern democrats filibustered for four weeks.

22—1911—FRANCIS E. W. HARPER died, noted anti-slavery lecturer.

23—1870—HIRAM R. REVELS, first Negro U. S. Senator elected from Mississippi, served to March 3rd, 1871.

24—1915—AMANDA SMITH died, great Evangelist born a slave in Maryland, 1837.

25—1870—HIRAM R. REVELS, of Mississippi was seated in the U. S. Congress.

26—1926—TIGER FLOWERS won middleweight championship from Harry Greb in 15 rounds, New York City.

27—1922—BERT A. WILLIAMS, great comedian collapsed on stage at Detroit, Michigan.

27—1939—MRS. FRANKLIN D. ROOSEVELT resigned from the D. A. R. because they refused to permit Marian Anderson, Negro contralto singer the right to sing in Constitution Hall.

28—1776 GENERAL GEORGE WASHINGTON wrote complimentary letter to Phyllis Wheatley, Negro poetess.

29—1860—GEORGE A. P. BRIDGETOWER died, great musician, prince and composer, buried in London, England,

29—1940—ROBERT S. ABBOTT, Publisher of the Chicago Defender, died in Chicago, Illinois.

MARCH

1—1919—NEAR RIOT—Birmingham, Alabama.
2—1932—KIDNAPING OF LINDBERGH BABY, body later found by William Allen.
3—1865—CONGRESS PASSED BILL freeing wives and children of Negro soldiers.
4—1922—BERT A. WILLIAMS died in New York City, greatest comedian of his time.
5—1770—CRISPUS ATTUCKS fell the first martyr of the massacre on Boston Common.
6—1943—300 WAR WORKERS in a factory at Wheeling, W. Va., voted to strike because a Negro had been hired.
7—1909—A month later MATTHEW HENSON made his final dash to North Pole with Perry.
8—1884—3 days later WILLIAM EDWARD SCOTT was born, Indianaolis, Indiana, great artist.
9—1871—OSCAR DePRIEST born Florence, Alabama, Chicago's first Negro Alderman and Congressman.
10—1913—HARRIET TUBMAN died, lecturer against slavery and underground railroad operator.
11—1921—SPRINGFIELD, OHIO race riot. A policeman and a Negro wounded.
12—1943—JIMMY BIVINS defeated Tami Mauriello in 10 rounds at Madison Square Garden, N. Y.
13—1938—FRIEND OF THE NEGRO, CLARENCE DARROW, died in Chicago, Illinois.
14—1935—RICHARD B. HARRISON, celebrated actor "De Lawd" of Green Pastures died in New York City.
15—1938—HENRY ARMSTRONG whipped Baby Arizmendi in ten rounds, Los Angeles, California.
16—1810—One day later, TOM MOLINEAUX, first black heavyweight American champion pugilist of America, was beaten by Tom Cribb in Ireland.
17—1898—EX-SENATOR BLANCHE K. BRUCE died in Washington, D. C., born in slavery.
18—1935—THE FUNERAL of Richard B. Harrison, actor and reader was held in Chicago, Illinois.

MARCH

19—1891—WEST VIRGINIA appropriated funds for building of Negro college.
20—1883—J. E. MATZELIGER, patented a shoe lasting machine, bought by the United Shoe Machine Co.
21—1923—C. M. WHITE died, Denver, Colorado, supreme commander, American Woodman.
22—1931—RICHARD B. HARRISON received Spingarn Medal from Lieut. Governor Lehman of New York.
23—ALEXANDER HAMILTON was the firct race man to go to the Continental Congress.
24—FOUR NEGROES have been registers of the U. S. Treasury.
25—1788—TRAFFIC IN SLAVERY was prohibited in the State of Massachusetts.
26—1831—RICHARD ALLEN, founder of A. M. E. Church, and its first bishop died.
27—1943—3 days later GEORGE W. REYNOLDS and his white sweetheart Lucile D'Aprano were found murdered near Akron, Ohio.
28—1938—U. S. SUPREME COURT by decision of 6 to 2 decided Negroes had right to picket stores for jobs.
29—1870—3 days later THOMAS PETERSON was first Negro to vote after ratification of 15th Amendment.
30—1938—HENRY ARMSTRONG knocked out Lew Feldman in the 5th round in New York City.
31—1871—JACK JOHNSON born in Galveston, Texas.
31—1891—GEORGE DIXON won featherweight championship from Cal McCarthy by K.O. in 22 rounds, Troy, N. Y.
31—1939—PRESIDENT FRANKLIN D. ROOSEVELT extended cordial greetings to George W. Carver, noted Negro scientist at Tuskegee Institute, Tuskegee, Ala.

APRIL

1—1938—JOE LOUIS knocked out Harry Thomas in 5th round, Chicago, Illinois.

2—1938—THEODORE HENDERSON, 15 of Cincinnati, Ohio, won 1st prize in Peace Poster Contest from 1700 entries in 44 states.

3—1589—SAINT BENEDICT, the Moore Negro Saint of Catholic Church, died.

4—1938—ENDING OF first Negro Business Exposition in Chicago, Illinois.

5—1865—BOOKER T. WASHINGTON, founder of Tuskegee Institute was born a slave in Virginia.

6—1909—MATTHEW A. HENSON helped Admiral Robert E. Perry put U. S. flag on North Pole.

7—1872—JOE WALCOTT was born in Barbadoes, West Indies, welterweight champion of the world.

8—1938—3 days previous Congressman HAMILTON FISH introduced bill for army and navy equality for Negroes.

9—1898—PAUL ROBESON was born, Princeton, N. J. First A.M.E. Church organized 1816 by Richard Allen.

10—1938—FUNERAL of Ex U. S. Congressman, Thomas E. Miller, age 88, Charleston, S. C., died April 7, 1938.

11—1906—ROY TIGER WILLIAMS, pugilist, born 1906.

12—1938—WALTER WHITE and Delegation visited President Roosevelt, urged him to stop lynching.

13—1938—ARTHUR W. MITCHELL nominated on Democratic ticket for 3rd term in U. S. Congress.

14—1775—FIRST ABOLITION Society in America organized.

14—1940—BOOKER T. WASHINGTON Postage Stamps went on sale — first time an American Negro had been so honored.

15—1865—ABRAHAM LINCOLN, President and Emancipator of black slaves died.

16—1862—SLAVERY ABOLISHED in Dist. of Columbia.

17—1787—RICHARD ALLEN was organizing African Church in Pennsylvania.

APRIL

18—1890—On the 2nd day of this month GEORGIA ceded a part of her slave state to the Union.

19—1938—THOMAS A. DORSEY is America's foremost Gospel song composer.

20—1938—Robert Ripley said DUKE ELLINGTON could play three and one-half days continously using only his own compositions.

21—1899—First of this month JOHN MERRICK and A. W. MOORE organized North Carolina Mutual Life Insurance Co., Durham, N. C.

22—1915—On 5th of this month JACK JOHNSON was knocked out in 26 rounds by Jess Willard at Havana, Cuba.

23—1856—GRANVILLE T. WOODS, inventer of telephone receiver and telegraphic induction was born, Columbus, Ohio.

23—1940—WALTER BARNES, orchestra leader and 200 others were burned to death in America's worst dance hall disaster in Natchez, Miss.

24—1862—TREATY SIGNED between America and England for suppression of slave trade.

25—1938—THREE WHITE YOUTHS electrocuted in Belefonte, Pa., prison for 41 cents hold-up, slaying of Negro, Floyd Tranon.

26—1890—SHERIDAN A. BRUSEAUX, Detective head of Chicago Keystone Detective Agency, born at Little Rock, Arkansas.

27—1803—TOUSSAINT L'OVERTURE died at Besancan, France, soldier, statesman, liberator.

28—1802—Two days later, ALEXANDER DUMAS, France's greatest novelist was born.

29—1923—DR. A. M. MOORE, co-founder of North Carolina Mutual Life Insurance Co., died.

30—1900—WRECK OF CASEY JONE'S train at Vaughn, Miss., Sim Webb, Negro, was fireman.

31—1926—Yesterday, BESSIE COLEMAN, famed aviatrix, fell 5300 feet and was killed at Jacksonville, Fla.

MAY

1—On 12th of this month, 1932, WILLIAM ALLEN, Negro truck driver, found dead body of kidnaped Lindberg baby.

2—1879—NANNIE BURROUGHS was born, Culpepper, Va., educator, orator.

3—1884—A day later FANNIE M. SMITH, Washington, died at Tuskegee, Alabama.

4—1938—JULIAN D. STEELE, Negro, married Mary Bradley Dawes, relative of vice president Dawes, in Boston.

5—1865—CLAYTON POWELL, born Franklin Co. Va., clergyman and author.

6—1857—DRED SCOTT decision by the U. S. Supreme Court, "Negroes have no rights that white man must respect."

7—1922—Two days later, R. T. GRENER, first Negro graduate of Harvard University died in Chicago.

8—1915—BISHOP HENRY M. TURNER of the African Methodist Episcopal Church died.

9—1930—JACK THOMPSON won welterweight title from Jackie Fields, Detroit, Michigan.

10—1919—JAMES REESE EUROPE died in New York City, most noted band leader of 369th Regiment band.

11—1924—H. A. RUCKER, former collector of Internal Revenue, Georgia, died in Atlanta, Ga.

12—1901—JOE GANS won lightweight championship from Frank Erne, at Fort Erie, Ontario, Canada.

13—1914—JOE LOUIS was born in Alabama, hard hitting heavyweight champion of the world.

14—1938—IN ITALY 80,000 boo America for her refusal to recognize Mussolini's conquest of Ethiopia.

15—1918—HENRY JOHNSON and NEEDHAM ROBERTS, whipped a German raiding party of 20, were first soldiers to be decorated.

16—1899—BOOKER T. WASHINGTON received invitation to speak to citizens of Charleston, W. Va.

14

MAY

17—1864—BLIND BOONE was born Miami, Missouri, great musical prodigy.

17—1942—BILL ROBINSON, celebrated tap dancer auctioned off a pair of his shoes at a Bond party at the "Chez Paree" in Chicago. The shoes were bought by Lewis A. Weiss for $30,000.

18—1936—JOHN G. ROBINSON, Great Aviator, landed in New York, fresh from Ethiopia, where he fought against Italy.

19—1938—GROVER NASH of Chicago, commissioned to fly air mail, air mail week, first Negro so honored.

20—1746—TOUSSAINT L'OVERTURE, Soldier and Liberator of Haiti was born.

21—1833—OBERLIN COLLEGE issued welcome to Negro students.

22—1917—E. T. PIERSON, lynched by white mob near Memphis, Tennessee.

23—1854—One day later, LINCOLN UNIVERSITY of Chester, Pa., was founded for Negroes.

24—1879—WILLIAM LLOYD GARRISON, great Abolutionist and friend of the Negro, died in New York City, age 74.

25—1849—THOMAS GREENE BETHUNE, Blind Tom, was born in slavery, world's greatest blind musician.

26—1826—JOHN B. RUSSWORM of Bowdoin College, was first Negro to graduate in America.

27—1863—NEGRO SOLDIERS at Port Hudson, under Col. Nelson, startled the world by their bravery.

28—1896—BOOKER T. WASHINGTON selected for Honorary Degree by Harvard University.

29—JAPAN AND MANY other Countries have acquired Agricultrists from Tuskegee Institute.

30—1903—COUNTEE CULLEN was born, Editor and Poet.

31—1936—HENRY ARMSTRONG, featherweight champion, won welterweight title from Barney Ross, 15 rounds, New York City.

JUNE

1—1859—HENRY O. TANNER, born Pittsburgh, Pa., great artist, died Paris, France.

2—1921—Yesterday ending of RACE RIOTS in Tulsa, Oklahoma, 10 whites and 21 Negroes killed. Negro section burned.

3—1875—Two days previous BOOKER T. WASHINGTON graduated from Hampton Institute.

4—On 27th of this month, 1936, PERRY PARKER died, grand chairman Pullman Porters Benefit Association.

5—1917—To Sept. 12, 1918, 2,290,527 NEGROES registered for service in the U. S. army.

6—1863—NEGRO SOLDIERS fought bravely at Milliken's Bend.

7—1930—The successful PICKETING FOR JOBS was started in Chicago, Illinois.

8—1938—Two days previous, England passed a law to protect the property of Emperor HALLIE SELASSIE.

9—1799—2 days previous ALEXANDER PUSHKIN was born in Moscow, Russia, Russia's great black poet.

10—1914—On 27th of this month, JACK JOHNSON beat Frank Moran on points 20 rounds, Paris, France.

11—1938—JOHNNY WOODRUFF won 1938 intercollegiate A.A.A.A. Quarter and Half Mile Runs in New York City.

12—1938—A month previous, HALLIE SELASSIE said Ethiopa would fight Italy until they were exterminated.

13—1908—THOMAS GREENE BETHUNE, Blind Tom died, made fortune for three different families.

14—1938—One day later, LOTTIE KINSEY was acquitted by all white jury for killing J. Scott Padgett, white attacker, Walterboro, S. Carolina.

15—1920—DULUTH, MINNESOTA RIOT, 3 Negroes reported lynched.

16—1863—Second day of the assult on Petersburg, Va., led by BLACK TROOPS.

JUNE

17—1871—JAMES WELDON JOHNSON, born Jacksonville, Fla., diplomat, author, orator.

18—1929—AL BROWN won bantamweight championship from Vidal Gregorio in 15 rounds, New York.

19—1863—Second day of assult on Ft. Wagner, BLACK SOLDIERS fighting bravely.

20—1858—CHARLES W. CHESTNUT born Cleveland, Ohio, teacher, author.

21—1859—HENRY O. TANNER born Pittsburgh, Pa.. most distinguished Negro artist, died, Paris, France.

22—1937—JOE LOUIS won heavyweight championship from James J. Braddock, Chicago, Illinois.

23—1938—Yesterday, JOE LOUIS knocked out Max Schmelling in 2 minutes, 4 seconds, first round, New York City.

24—1938—One day later, JAMES WELDON JOHNSON, poet and educator, was killed in auto accident at Wiscasset, Maine.

25—1935—JOE LOUIS knocked out Primo Carnera in 6th round, Yankee Stadium, New York City.

26—1919—SOL BUTLER broke high jump record, Joinville, France.

27—1872—PAUL LAURANCE DUNBAR was born, Dayton, Ohio, America's greatest lyric poet.

28—1936—Yesterday, PERRY PARKER, chairman of Pullman Porters Benefit Association died.

29—1935—CORTEZ W. PETERS of Washington, D. C. won honors as world's second fastest typist, Chicago, Illinois.

30—1919—SUPREME LIBERTY Life Insurance Company founded by F. L. Gillespie, Chicago, Illinois.

JULY

1—1938—6 NEGRO POLICEMEN were made Sergeants in the Chicago Police Department.

2—1869—JAMES D. CORROTHERS, born in Michigan, Baptist Minister and poet of distinction.

3—1871—JOSEPH H. DOUGLASS, born in Washington, D. C., grandson of Frederick Douglass, great violinist.

4—1910—JACK JOHNSON knocked out James J. Jeffries, 15 rounds at Reno, Nevada.

5—1902—AL BROWN born in Panama, bantamweight champion of the world.

6—1863—BATTLE of MILLIKEN'S BEND, near Vicksburg, Negro soldiers fought gallantly.

7—1938—The body of an unnamed Negro was burned on the city dump in Rolling Fork, Miss.

8—1938—CLARENCE NORRIS, one of the Scottsboro boy's death sentence was commuted to life 3 days ago by Governor Bib Graves.

9—1938—JOHN DUKE, 60 year old Negro alleged murderer, was burned alive in Arabia, Georgia.

10—1898—9 days previous, GEORGE DIXON was defeated by Ben Jordan in 25 rounds at New York City.

11—1919—RACE RIOT, Longview, Texas, 4 white men wounded, Negro section burned.

12—In Randall Island Stadium, CORNELIUS JOHNSON and DAVE ALBRITTON jumped 6 ft. 9¾ inches, world's record.

13—1804—Yesterday, ALEXANDER HAMILTON died from wounds received in duel with Aaron Burr.

14—1938—3 days previous, GEORGE FITCH won Ten round decision over Steve Carr, New Haven, Conn., Gene Tuney, referee.

15—On 5th day of this month JESSIE OWENS. world's fastest runner, was married to Minnie Ruth Solomon, Cleveland, Ohio.

16—1863—Gallant NEGRO TROOPS bore the brunt of battle at Fort Wagner.

JULY

17—1891—HAILE SELASSIE was born King of Kings, conquering Lion of the Tribe of Judah.

18—4 NEGRO REGIMENTS were awarded Croix De Guerre for bravery in the World War.

19—To 23rd, 1919—RACE RIOT, Washington, D. C., 3 Negroes, 4 whites killed, 30 persons wounded.

20—1933—DR. ALBERT E. FORSYTHE and C. ALFRED ANDERSON, first Negroes to cross American continent in their own plane.

21—1933—RAS DESTA DEMPTU, son-in-law of Haile Selassie, dined at the White House with President Franklin D. Roosevelt.

22—1937—Opening of JONES BROTHER'S Ben Franklin 5c, 10c & $1.00 Store in Chicago, Ill.

23—1863—KELLY MILLER, University Dean, author, lecturer, born in Winnsboro, S. C.

24—1938—2 days previous CLAUDE BROOKS was lynched by a mob in Canton, Miss.

25—1935—LEONARD TYNER, 13 year old Negro boy of Chicago, marble champion of the world.

26—1892—PAUL E. JOHNSON, inventor of physiotherapy equipment, born in Atlanta, Ga.

27—1870—HENRY L. JOHNSON, born in Augusta, Ga., lawyer, politician, recorded of deeds.

28—1868—Adoption of the 14th AMENDMENT to the U. S. Constitution.

29—1870—GEORGE DIXON, born at Halifax, Nova Scotia, was both bantamweight and lightweight champion.

30—1938—One month ago TUSKEGEE INSTITUTE reported no lynchings for first 6 months of 1938.

31—1938—2 days previous JAKE POWELL, ball player of N. Y. Yankee, was suspended for 10 days by Judge Landis for using word "Nigger".

AUGUST

1—1887—JUNIUS C. AUSTIN, born in Virginia, great preacher and Race leader.

2—1911—ROBERT ALLEN COLE died in New York City, one of the world's greatest actors.

3—1924—BERLIN, GERMANY, Thousands visited the Sangerhausen Rosarium to see the world's first beautiful BLACK ROSE.

4—1919—RACE RIOT, Chicago, ended after 10 days, 16 whites, 22 Negroes killed, 600 wounded.

5—1895—TIGER FLOWERS, middleweight champion, was born at Camille, Georgia.

6—1919—JOHN MERRICK died, born in Clinton, N. C., successful business man.

7—1938—NEW YORK NEGROES win right to third of jobs in Harlem, decree by Uptown Chamber ot Commerce.

8—1866—MATTHEW A. HENSON, born at Charles County, Maryland, went with Peary to North Pole.

9—1936—4 days previous JESSIE OWENS ran 200 meters 20.7 seconds, new world's record, Berlin, Germany.

10—1885—ISSAC MURPHY, great Negro jocky, won Ten Thousand Dollar Match Race, rode Freedland against Woodford.

11—1873—J. ROSEMOND JOHNSON, born at Jacksonville, Fla., great music composer.

12—1922—Old Home of FREDERICK DOUGLASS dedicated as a nationtl shrine.

13—1938—WILLIE ELEY, Negro pugilist, died after being knocked out by Buzz Barton in Kingston, Jamaica.

14—On August 2nd 1933 — Ripley said, RALPH METCALFE had equalled or broken every standard sprinting record on earth.

15—1875—SAMUEL COLERIDGE TAYLOR, born in London, died Sept. 1st, 1912, distinguished composer.

16—1922—PROF. E. L. SIMON died at Atlanta, Ga., educator and business man.

AUGUST

17—1938—HENRY ARMSTRONG beat Lou Ambers in 15 rounds for lightweight title, New York City, now lightweight, featherweight and welterweight champion

18—1938—EATONVILLE, FLORIDA, is an all Negro town, its election is on this date, the town has no jail.

19—1791—Thomas Jefferson received the new Almanic from BENJAMIN BANNEKER, the great astronomer.

20—1938—2 months previous LEWIS WILLIAMS, Pullman porter, was the hero of the disasterous Olympian train wreck.

21—1831—NAT TURNER, leader of insurrection and preacher, started murdering slave owners in Virginia.

22—1791—Second day Revolution by TOUSSAINT L'-OVERTURE to free the black people of Haiti from France.

23—JOE LOUIS was first Negro to win world's heavyweight championship in America.

24—1778—Official report that there were an average of 35 NEGROES in each white Revolutionary Regiment.

25—1938—JOHN HENRY LEWIS knocked out Dominick Ceccarelli in third round at Nutley, N. J.

26—1867—ROBERT R. MOTON, born at Amelia County, Va., educator, president of Tuskegee Institute.

27—1935—JOE LOUIS shook hands with President Franklin D. Roosevelt at the White House, was congratulated on his victories.

28—1938—WILLIE (Suicide) JONES made parachute jump from plane at height of 29,400 feet, Chicago, Ill.

29—1924—A. J. STOKES died in California, great preacher and financier.

30—1791—Thomas Jefferson wrote BENJAMIN BANNEKER a letter thanking him for the Almanac he received.

31—1919—RACE RIOTS, Knoxville, Tenn., 1 Negro and 1 guardsman killed, 7 whites and 6 Negroes wounded.

SEPTEMBER

1—1822—HIRAM R. REVELS, first Colored Senator, born free, Fayetteville, N. C.

2—1938—Five PUGILISTIC CHAMPIONSHIPS are held by 3 Negroes who neither drink, chew, smoke nor gamble.

3—1906—JOE GANS beat Battling Nelson in 42 rounds on foul, Goldfield, Nevada.

4—1922—F. PRIDE died. He was a decorated captain of A. E. F. in World War.

5—1930—JACK THOMPSON lost to Tommy Freeman in 15 rounds.

6—1901—JAMES PARKER knocked down Czolgosz when he shot President William McKinley at Buffalo, New York.

7—1817—PAUL CUFFEE died, ship builder, skipper and African colonizer.

8—1892—Two days previous GEORGE DIXON stopped Jack Skelly in New Orleans, La.

9—1908—JOE GANS beaten by Battling Nelson in 21 rounds at Colma, Calif.

10—1847—JOHN R. LYNCH, born at Concordia, Ala., statesman and member of 43rd and 44th Congress.

11—1932—WILLIAM E. LILLY was first Negro to write standard volume on Life of Lincoln.

12—1913—JESSIE OWENS was born, fastest runner in the world.

13—1886—LEROY ALAIN LOCKE, born at Philadelphia, Pa., author and educator.

14—1790—A SOCIETY for the abolition of slavery was organized in Connecticut.

15—1854—DR. JOSEPH WILLIS died, he organized the first Baptist Church of Louisiana.

16—1510—GUINEA and HAITI, like many other countries began their traffic in slaves.

17—MOSES married an Ethiopian woman. See bible, Numbers 12:1.

SEPTEMBER

18—1895—BOOKER T. WASHINGTON delivered masterpiece at the Atlanta Exposition.

19—1923—S. X. FLOYD died at Augusta, Ga., minister and educator.

20—1897—MAJOR TAYLOR, world's champion cycalist, won great one-mile race at Waverly, N. J.

21—1933—Yesterday WILLIAM WALKER, great jockey, died in Louisville, Ky., rode Ten Broeck in his triumph over Mollie McCarthy.

22—1862—LINCOLN issued proclaimation offering to pay for slaves and colonize them in Africa or America.

23—1839—A New Orleans SLAVE SHIP was captured on the African coast by Great Britian.

24—1922—BATTLING SIKI (Senagalese) knocked out George Carpentier in 6 rounds, Paris, France.

25—1826—South Carolina had its first SLAVE INSURRECTION.

26—1919—2 days later RACE RIOTS, Omaha, Nebr., 1 Negro lynched, court house burned, Mayor badly beaten.

27—1827—HIRAM R. REVELS was born in Fayetteville, N. C., minister, U. S. Senator and philosopher.

28—1864—RICHARD B. HARRISON was born in Canada, reader and celebrated actor.

29—1918—PRIVATE TILLMAN WEBSTER, 371, Inf., Ardenil, France, crawled 200 yards under fire and rescued wounded officer.

30—1938—CHICAGO NEGROES started picketing movie theaters for jobs for race movie machine operators.

OCTOBER

1—1800—NAT TURNER, born at South Hampton, Va., the great insurrectionist.

2—1858—Attorney General ruled SLAVES could not take out patents on their own inventions.

3—1919—RACE RIOTS, Elaine, Arkansas ended after 3 days, 5 whites and 18 Negroes killed.

4—1831—NAT TURNER, the insurrectionist, was hanged.

5—1872—BOOKER T. WASHINGTON left his home to matriculate in Hampton Institute.

6—1895—BOOKER T. WASHINGTON received thousands of congratulations for his Atlanta speech.

7—1821—WILLIAM STILL, born in New Jersey, official of Underground Railroad.

8—1893—BOOKER T. WASHINGTON married his third wife, Maggie James Murray.

9—1930—After 4 months of picketing, the Woolworth Stores put COLORED GIRLS in Chicago Stores.

10—JULIUS ROSENWALD, the generous Jew, helped build 2,500 schools before his death.

11—1882—NATHANIEL R. DETT, born at Drummondsville, Ont., composer, author of "Listen To The Lambs".

12—1492—PETRO ALONZA, black navigator, was co-discoverer of America with Christopher Columbus.

13—1863—The tide of the Civil War changed with the enlistment of NEGRO SOLDIERS.

14—1922—J. E. JONES died at Richmond, Va., educator and theological teacher.

15—1870—The C. M. E. CHURCH was organized in Tenn.

16—1859—JOHN BROWN raided Harpers Ferry, Va., in his attempt to free the black slaves.

17—1909—JACK JOHNSON knocked out Stanley Keichell in 12 rounds, Colma, California.

18—1898—The NORTH CAROLINA MUTUAL LIFE INSURANCE CO. was organized in Durham, N. C.

OCTOBER

19—1886—A Negro, WILLEY JONES, was first street car line operator in Pine Bluff, Arkansas.

20—1785—DAVID WALKER won critism from his own people by attacking slavery through the press.

21—1922—J. A. SCOTT died in Chicago, Ill., lawyer and race patriot.

22—1852—T. J. HORNSBY was born, preacher and founder of Pilgrim Life Insurance Co. of Augusta, Ga.

23—1818—Uprising and rebellion of slaves at Charleston, South Carolina.

24—1814—N. Y. authorized raising of 2 BLACK REGIMENTS to fight at Sacketts Harbor War, 1812.

25—FREDERICK DOUGLASS is buried in Rochester, New York.

26—1775—PHYLLIS WHEATLEY, race poet, wrote George Washington Letters of Advice during the war.

27—1886—CUBA passed a law abolishing slavery.

28—1940—Over 25,000 NEGRO GRADUATES come out of our schools that year.

29—1864—The Confederacy enlisted BLACK TROOPS just before Lee's surrender.

30—1937—TUSKEGEE INSTITUTE has nearly 2500 acres of land.

31—1904—JOE GANS whipped Jimmie Britt in 5 rounds at San Francisco, Calif.

NOVEMBER

1—1743—TOUSSAINT L'OUVERTURE was born a slave in San Domingo, great statesman and soldier.

2—A NEGRO'S PATRIOTISM outweighs his privileges by at least eighty percent.

3—1920—OCOEE, FLORIDA ELECTION DAY RIOT, would not let Negroes vote, 2 whites killed, 1 Negro lynched.

4—1941—REV. A. CLAYTON POWELL Jr., first Negro to be elected Councilman of New York City.

5—1939—FUNERAL OF MAJOR JOHN R. LYNCH held in Chicago, was Congressman from 1873 to 1877, from Mississippi.

6—1768—ABSALOM JONES, born in Delaware, preacher and co-founder of the A. M. E. Church.

7—1938—MOUND BAYOU, MISS., all Negro town, is quiet and has no jail.

8—NAT TURNER, insurrectionist and FREDERICK DOUGLASS, abolitionist, were both preachers.

9—1731—BENJAMIN BANNEKER born at Balto County, Md., noted astronomer, inventer of America's striking clock.

10—The South lost the war largely because they had no soldiers to compete with the BLACK UNION SOLDIERS.

11—Half of the lynchings of black people never get to the press.

12—1862—PRELIMINARY EMANCIPATION PROCLAMATION by Lincoln was issued on Sept. 22nd.

13—1913—DR. DANIEL WILLIAMS, famous Chicago surgeon, first to stitch the human heart.

14—1915—BOOKER T. WASHINGTON, founder of Greater Tuskegee Institute, died.

15—218 B. C.—HANNIBAL, world's greatest general, marched through Spain and France crossing the Alps.

16—1865—Over 65,000 NEGROES helped the Confederate army directly or indirectly.

NOVEMBER

17—1937—Since 1882 Georgia has lynched over 572 Negroes.

18—GEORGE DIXON, featherweight champion pugilist, is buried in Boston, Mass.

19—1878—CHARLES S. GILPIN, born at Richmond, Va., great actor, starred in "Emperor Jones".

20—1732—CAPTAIN HARRY DEAN was born, author of "Pedro Garrino".

21—1937—This year seven prominent white men have been found dead in homes of COLORED WOMEN.

22—1938—BILL ROBINSON, past 50 years old, is still champion tap dancer.

23—JOHN BROWN, the abolitionist, kissed a Negro baby just before he was hanged.

24—1870—ROBERT S. ABBOTT was born in Savannah, Ga., editor-owner The Chicago Defender.

25—1874—JOE GANS, born at Baltimore, Md., lightweight champion of the world.

26—1938—NEGROES live and have schools and churches on top of Lookout Mountain, Chattanooga, Tenn.

27—1883—One day previous, SOJOURNER TRUTH died at Battle Creek, Mich., Orator and abolitionist.

28—OKLAHOMA prohibited Negroes marrying Indians as soon as the Indians became wealthy by oil wells.

29—1863—THE BLACK WOMAN'S BURDEN was carrying the bastard child of her cruel slave master.

30—1922—KING TUT-ANKH-AMEN'S tomb was found in the Valley of Kings, on the west bank of the Nile at Luxor. His body was in pure gold coffin.

31—Much of MAMMOTH CAVE in Kentucky was discovered by black people.

DECEMBER

1—1859—A day later JOHN BROWN (white), the abolitionist, was hanged for his raid on Harpers Ferry, Va.

2—1866—HARRY T. BURLEIGH, born at Erie, Pa., soloist, composer of "Deep River".

3—1926—TIGER FLOWERS lost middleweight title to Mickey Walker, 10 rounds, Chicago.

4—1833—PHILADELPHIA was host to first Anti-Slavery Convention.

5—1784—PHILLIS WHEATLEY died, born in Africa, enslaved here, greatest poet of her time, age 41.

6—1934—Yesterday ITALIAN TROOPS started war on Ethiopians in Wal Wal, Ethiopia.

7—1864 MYRTILLA MINER died, built school to train Negro teachers, Washington, D. C.

8—1935—ANGELO HERNDON released on bond by Judge Dorsey from Fullerton Tower jail in Georgia.

9—All high honors in horsemanship and marksmanship have been held by NEGRO SOLDIERS.

10—1846—NORBERT RILLIEUX of Louisiana, invented a sugar refining process.

11—1917—HOUSTON, TEXAS RIOTS, five soldiers of 24th Infantry were executed by the U. S. Government.

12—1912—HENRY ARMSTRONG, featherweight and welterweight champion, was born in St. Louis. Mo.

13—1920—Three days later INDEPENDENCE, KANSAS RIOT, 1 white and 1 Negro killed, 3 whites wounded.

14—1915—COL. WM. J. SIMMONS organized the New Ku Klux Klan to stop Negro progress.

15—1925—BATTLING SIKI was killed in Hell's Kitchen, New York City.

16—1937—Ripley said "JOHN HENRY LEWIS is great grand nephew of Tom Molineaux, first heavyweight champ, son of fighter and 2 fighting brothers."

17—1862—Yesterday SLAVERY was abolished in the District of Columbia by Congress.

18—1901—JOE WALCOTT knocked out Rube Ferns in 5 rounds, Toronto, Canada.

DECEMBER

19—1875—CARTER G. WOODSON, born at New Canton, Va., great historian and editor.

20—1865—2 days previous, Congress adopted 13TH AMENDMENT to the U. S. Constitution.

21—Many SLAVE CHILDREN were compelled to nurse the cancerous breasts of their white mistresses.

22—1826—J. A. HANDY born in Baltimore, Md., orator and Bishop of A. M. E. Church.

23—1906 CORTEZ W. PETERS, born Washington, D. C. World's Champion Typist.

24—1881—H. H. GARNET died in Monrovia, West Africa, preacher and missionary.

25—1835—B. T. TANNER born in Philadelphia, Pa. Bishop of the A. M. E. Church.

26—1908—JACK JOHNSON defeated Tommy Burns for heavyweight title in 14 rounds, Sidney, Australia.

27—1891—H. BINGA DISMOND born in Richmond, Va., world's champion runner.

28—1810—TOMMY LAFON was born free in New Orleans, La., philanthropist, school teacher and merchant.

29—1898—JULIUS C. BLEDSOE born at Waco, Texas, first Negro to enter grand opera.

30—1775—Enlistment of BLACK SOLDIERS in Revolutionary War ordered by George Washington.

31—MRS. COX, a maid, was bequeathed $50,000.00 by Marie Dressler, has built a fine roadhouse in Savannah, Georgia.

31—1942—PROF. J. WESLEY JONES first Negro to become Assistant Supt. of Mails, Chicago, Ill.

MY PEOPLE FROM A TO Z

ASKIA—Emperor of Songhay, ruled from Atlantic Ocean to Lake Chad, Capitol, Timbuctoo.

ABRAH—Black Slave, started Christain War that lasted a thousand years and wrecked Roman Empire.

ARMSTRONG, HENRY—Feather, Light and Welterweight Champion of the world.

AESOP—World's greatest fabulist—620 B. C.

ALONZO, PETRO—Navigator and Co-discoverer of America, with Columbus.

ATTUCKS, CRISPUS—First martyr in the Revolutionary War.

ANDERSON, J. O.—Co-inventor of the world's first mechanical reaper.

ALLEN, RICHARD—Founder of the African Methodist Episcopal Church.

AUSTIN, JUNIUS C.—Internationally known Baptist preacher.

BARCA, HAMICAR—Chief of Carthaginian Army—247 B. C.

BANNEKER, BENJAMIN—Astronomer, inventor of calendar and first striking clock.

BERNADOTTE—From Pav, founded royal family of Sweden, was ruler in 1818.

BATISTA, FULGENICO—Leader of Cuban revolt in 1933 head of their great army.

BETHUNE, THOMAS GREENE (Blind Tom)—World's greatest blind painist.

BEETHOVEN—World's greatest musician and composer.

BEAVERS, LOUISE—Noted Hollywood screen star.

CYRENE, SIMON—Helped Christ carry His cross up Mount Calvary.

COLEMAN, BESSIE—First great Race aviatrix.

CUSH—Begat Nimrod, he began to be a mighty one in the earth—Bible, Genesis 10:8

CATEWAYO—King of Zulu Land, killed Prince Napoleon and wiped out entire British army—1879.

CARVER, GEORGE W.—America's foremost chemist Tuskegee Institute.

DeSAIBLE, JEAN BAPTISTE POINT—First settler in Chicago—1779.

DUMAS, ALEXANDRA—Celebrated French novelist.

DOUGLASS, FREDERICK—Abolutionist, orator and statesman.

DIXON, GEORGE—World's champion featherweight pugilist.

DODDS, GENERAL ALFRED—A Senegalese, was commander of French army in 1901.

DUNBAR, PAUL LAURENCE—Greatest poet of his race.

DETT, NATHANIEL—Renowned musical composer, author of "Listen To The Lambs".

DUBOIS, W. E. B.—Economist, sociologist and thinker.

DAWSON, CHARLES—Famous Afro-American artist.

ESTEVANICO—Tireless explorer and discoverer of Arizona and New Mexico.

EUROPE, JAMES R.—Great bandmaster of the old 15th N. Y. Regiment Band.

ELLINGTON, DUKE—Famous orchestra leader.

FLIPPER, HENRY O.—Soldier, graduate of West Point.

FALASHES—Black Jews of Abyssinia claim to be the original Jews.

FAGAN—Was the name of an American Negro who led Fillipinos against the U. S. in 1899.

FLOWERS, TIGER (Deacon)—World's champion middle weight pugilist.

FULLER, META WARRICK—Sculpture of note.

FULLER, THOMAS—Unlettered slave of Virginia, perhaps the world's greatest calculator.

GANS, JOE (Old Master)—World's lightweight champion pugilist.

GROVES, JUNIUS G. —America's potato king, of Kansas.

GARVEY, MARCUS—Organizer and founder of the U. N. I. A.

GREEN, WENDELL E.—Famous Chicago criminal lawyer.

HANNIBAL—Father of military strategy who defeated Rome.

HARVARD, CLAUDE—Mechanical wizzard of the Ford Plant, his sorting machine measures to 1/10,000th of an inch.

HENSON, MATTHEW—Explorer, went to North Pole with Commodore Perry.

HARRISON, HUBERT—America's greatest street speaker and lecturer of N. Y. City Board of Education.

HAYES, ROLAND—World's greatest lyric tenor singer.

INIHOTEP—Ancient Egyptian, father of medicine.

JACKSON, PETER—Great heavyweight pugilist of Australia.

JENKINS, MME.—Inventor of Aunt Jemima's Pancake Flour.

JOHN,"VI"—King of Portugal, ruled Portugal from Brazil.

JOHNSON, JACK—Cleverest world's heavyweight champion pugilist.

KHUFU, (Cheops)—Builder of the pyramids at Gizeh, 4,000 B. C., 2,500,000 blocks of granite.

KNOX, GEORGE L.—One of the first Race newspaper publishers.

KING, Wm. E.—Lawyer and State Senator of Illinois.

LATINO, JUAN—African poet of the 16th century.

LOUIS, JOE—World's heavyweight champion pugilist.

L'OVERTURE, TOUSSAINT—Of Haiti, greatest soldier of his day.

LANGSTON, JOHN M.—U. S. Congressman from Virginia.

MOLINEAUX, TOM—First American champion pugilist.

McCOY, ELIJAH—Famous inventor of the Lubricator.

MATZELIGER, J. ERNEST—Inventor of Shoe Lasting Machine.

MENELIK, II—Emperor and liberator of Ethiopia from Italy in 1896.

MALONE, ANNIE M.—Manufacturer of Poro Cosmetic Preparations.

MILLER, KELLY—Writer, author, thinker.

METCALFE, RALPH—Has broken or equalled every sprint record in the world.

MURPHY, ISAAC—Great jockey, won Kentucky Derby three times.

MELCHIADES—Pope 311-321, led Christianity to victory over Roman Empire.

MORTENOL, S. H.—Black commander of Paris, located and destroyed Germany's Big Bertha guns.

MORTENOL, S.H.—Commander of Paris from 1916-1918, 250 planes and 10,000 white men under him.

MULEY, ISHAMEL—Emperor of Morocco, had 25,000 white slaves and 12,000 horses, died in 1727.

MURRAY, CHARLES D.—Manufacturer of cosmetical goods, Chicago.

NEFERT—Egyptian Princess, 3,000 B. C.

NASH, CHARLES E. —U. S. Congressman from Louisiana.

NORFOLK, KID—Popular pugilist of his time.

O'HARA, JAMES E.—U. S. Congressman from North Carolina.

OWENS, JESSE—World's fastest runner

OWEN, CHANDLER—Journalist, orator, thinker.

PEDRO, I.—First Emperor of Brazil.

PUSHKIN, ALEXANDER S.—Russia's Premiere Black poet.

PEDRO, I—Son of John VI, First Emperor of Brazil, 1822 Married sister of Napoleon's second wife.

PEDRO, I.—His daughter, Queen of Portugal, sister-in-law of Queen Victoria of England.

PARKER, J. H.—Founder of Parker House Sausage Co., Chicago, Ill.

PARKER, JAMES—Knocked down Czolgosz when he shot President Wm. McKinley.

PICKENS, WILLIAM—Writer, organizer, orator of note.

POLLARD, FRITZ—Celerated football player.

PAGE, SATCHELL—Famous baseball pitcher.

QUINN, J. W.—Louisiana State Legislator, 1871-1872.

QUEEN OF SHEBA—Related to Cush, King Solomon and Haile Selassie.

QUETZALCOATL—Was the much worshipped Black God of Mexico.

ROGERS, J. A.—World traveler and famous historian.

REVELS, HIRAM R.—First Afro-American U.S. Senator.

RANDOLPH, A. PHILLIP—Silver-tongued orator and organizer.

ROBB, FREDERICK—Debator, lawyer and historian.

SAMPSON, BEACH—Slaughtered British soldier with sythe at Battle of Brandywine.

SPAULDING, C. C.—North Carolina banker and business man.

SODER, THOMAS W.—President and founder of John Brown organization, his work consist of getting better jobs for Negroes.

SAINT GELASIUS—Lived in 496, A. D.

SAINT MAURICE—Celestial Saint of Germany, Commander Roman Legion at Gaul.

SOLOMOM, KING—Related to Cush, Ham and Nimrod.

SCARBOROUGH, W. S.—Professor and teacher of Greek.

SELASSIE, HAILE—Once dethroned emperor of Ethiopia.

SIMMONS, ROSCOE—Eloquent Afro-American orator.

SISSLE, NOBLE—Composer and orchestra leader.

SANDERS, CALVIN—First in Chicago's job picketing campaign.

TROTTER, MONROE—Publisher and equial rights advocate.

TRUTH, SOJOURNER—Fearless abolutionist orator.

TUBMAN, HARRIET—Tireless anti-slavery agitator.

TUT-ANKH-AMEN, KING—Was Negroid, the most remarkable of the Pharaohs.

TAYLOR, COLERIDGE—Noted musical composer.

TOLAN, EDDIE—Famed world's champion runner.

TURNER, NAT—Early insurrectionist of 1831.

THORNTON, BEN—Famous detective, Indianapolis, Ind.

TAYLOR, MAJOR—World's champion cycalist.

TANNER, HENRY O.—Greatest artist of his Race.

USAPHIAS—High ranking King of Egypt.

VESEY, DENMARK—South Carolina anti-slavery insurrectionist.

VARICK, WILLIAM E.—A street in New York is named after this pioneer Negro.

VICTOR—Pope of Rome, was an African, 189-199, A. D.

VASCONCELOS, JOSE—Popular poet of the African Congo about 1710.

VERNON, W. T.—Bishop and Ex-Register of U. S. Treasure.

WHEATLEY, PHYLLIS—Great African born poet enslaved in America.

WOODS, GRANVILLE T.—Inventor of telephone receiver and 300 other patents.

WASHINGTON, BOOKER T.—Famous founder of Tuskegee Institute.

WILLIAMS, L. K.—Preacher and President of National Baptist Convention.

WILLIAMS, BERT—Greatest American comedian.

WALKER, GEORGE—Great actor, partner of Bert Williams.

WALCOTT, JOE—World's welterweight champion pugilist.

WALKER, MRS. C. J.—Manufacturer of cosmetics.

WOODSON, CARTER G.—Great historian of the darker races.

XAVIER, FRANCIOS—Freeman of Orleans Parish, La.

YEARBROUGH, PROF. ISAAC—Noted blind choir leader

YUSUF—King of Upper Sengel Africa.

YOUNG, CHARLES—Famous soldier and Colonel of U. S. army.

ZERAH—Victorious war king of Africa.

ZAUDITU, WAIZERU—Former Empress of Ethiopia.

DOROTHY MAYNOR—Noted Concert Singer.

CHAPLAIN L. M. FULLER—"Truth telling" Preacher, U. S. Army.

DOROTHY DONEGAN—Pianist of great talent.

"BEAU JACK"—From boot black to worlds champion boxer.

LENA HORNE—Hollywood Screen and Stage Star.

BOB MONTGOMERY—Lightweight Champion of the world.

35

KINGS AND QUEENS OF AFRICAN DESCENT

CUSH—Founded Ethiopia about 6280, or over 8200 years ago.

KING MENELIK II.—Liberator of Ethiopia from Italy, 1896.

KING TIRHAQUAH—Early ruler of Ethiopia. (bible).

KING PIANKHI—Ruled 721 B. C., conquered Egypt to the mouth of the Nile.

KING TAHARKA—Held thrones in both Ethiopia and Assyria.

SABACON—Established the 25th Ethiopian dynasty.

ORI—King of Ethiopia ruled the throne in 4470 B. C.

HALLIE SALASSIE II.—Was the 335th ruler of Ethiopia. since King Ori.

MENNOK—Was King of Ethiopia in 1270 B. C.

NIMROD—Son of Cush, was founder of Assyrian empire.

TRHAQUAH—Ruler of Ethiopia.

KING PIANKHI, I.—of Ethiopia, 721 B. C. conquered Egypt for Ethiopia.

KING MENNON—of Ethiopia, 1270, B. C. had army of 200,000, aided his uncle Priam in great Trojan war.

ZERA, King of Ethiopia, 944 B. C. invaded Egypt with army of one million men—bible.

KING CANDACE III.—Of Ethiopia 20 B. C. invaded Egypt and pillaged Thebes.

DUKE KWESI KVNTU—Reigns in Asbuasi, Ashanti, Gold Coast, West Africa.

PRINCE ADEBOOKLAMI—Of Abeokutah, Nigeria, Africa.

EMPRESS MENNEN—Empress of Ethiopia.

YOUSEF I, SENGALESE MONARK—11th Century, crossed Strait of Gibraltar, whipped European army 3 times.

AKHENATON—Richest man on earth, father of Tut-Ankh-Amen.

QUEEN NEFERTITI—Wife of Akenaton, said to be her brother, then rulers were marrying their sisters.

KING ABRAHA—Ruler of Ethiopia, accepted christianity, 330 A. D. started war that lasted 1000 years.

DUKE ALESSANDRO DE MEDCI—Duke of Florence, his family produced three Popes and three Kings of France.

TOMBUT—King of Guinea, on the West Coast of Africa very wealthy lived in 18th Century.

MULAI ISMALL—King of Morocco 18th century had 25,000 white slaves—his mother was a slave.

CHAKA ZULU MONARCH—Born 1786—most heartless of all rulers.

BEHANZIN HOSSU BOWELE—12th century potentate of West Africa sat on the throne of pure gold.

MOSESH—King of the Basutos of South Africa, 18th century beat England's best generals in war.

KING PREMPEH—Kwak Dua, III, Gold Coast King of the Ashantis, and a conquering warrior.

PRINCE THAMI GLAOUI—Morocco chief with 12,000 men under arms visited France in 1931.

CLITUS—King of Bactra and Cavalry General of Alexander, the great.

DON PEDRO II,—Emperor and Emancipator of Brazil.

ANNA ZINGHA—Beautiful queen of Matamba.

AFRICA—With the exception of Asia is the largest continent in the world—it is over three times as large as Australia, more than half again as large as South America and three times as large as the United States, including Alaska and outlying colonies. Africa contains one fifth of all the land upon the earth.

NEGRO INVENTORS AND THEIR PATENTS

HERBERT DUNN—Chicago, toy airplane.

WILLIAM DOUGLAS—Arkansas, harvesting machine has obtained many patents.

ROSS D. BROWN—Ind., Automatic glass gathering machine, patented Dec. 18th, 1906, patented Nov. 17th, 1908, patented June 7th, 1910.

JAMES DOYLE—Pittsburgh, Pa., restaurant self serving device.

ANDREW H. BEARD—Ala., Automatic "Jennie" car coupling device.

JOHN T. ROBINSON—Pa., ironing board.

GEORGE W. MURPHY—S. C., farm implements.

JAMES WHITE—Fla., Carpenters Rule.

LEROY M. HARDEN—Chicago, adjustable can opener.

ROBERT RILLIEUX—Ala., evaporating pan for refining sugar.

ROBERT A. PELHAM—Michigan, statistical tabulating machine.

BISHOP MONTGOMERY—Ala., fish scaling device.

JAMES FORTEN—Pa., devise for recording sales.

ALONZO A. MOORE—Mass, swimming learning machine.

ALFRED NEAL—Texas, excavating machine.

CHARLES H. JACKSON—Boston, 360 foot deep sea diving suit.

GARRETT A. MORGAN—Ohio, smoke and gas protector used by U. S. soldiers and allies in world war.

WILLIAM L. SMITH—Md., Oyster shucker and plastering machine.

ROBERT B. LEWIS—Maine, Oakum picking machine.

THE COTTON GIN—Is also said to have been the invention of a black slave.

LEWIS L. LATTERMAN—Ohio, electric motors and dynamos.

CHARLES A. GREENE, N. Y.—Chiropodist case.

THOMAS C. CRENSHAW—Chicago, Ill., June 1937, Direction Signal Control.

BENJAMIN A. CRENSHAW—Chicago, Ill., Nov. 1928, Signaling Device.

C. J. PERRY—Ohio, smoke consuming device.

GRANVILLE T. WOODS—Inventor of telephone receiver and many other devices.

JO. ANDERSON—A slave of Cyrus McCormick, inventor of world's first mechanical reaper.

LEWIS STEWART—Los Angeles. inventor of refillable fuse plug.

J. ERNEST METZELINGER—Inventor of first automatic shoe lasting machine.

ELIJAH McCOY—Detroit, inventor of lubricator, 47 U.S. patents, 10 in Europe.

MME. JENKINS—Aunt Jemima's pan cake flour.

ELBERT R. ROBINSON—Chicago, invented the groove street car rail.

ROBERT H. PENNINGTON—Mo. railroad signal system.

CLARENCE GREGG—Kansas City, Kas., machine gun carrying 14,000 cartridges.

C. V. PERRY—Washington, D. C.—Solutions for fire proofing fabric.

ROBERT PELHAM—Detroit, tabulating device used by U. S. Government.

WILLIAM B. PURVIS—Philadelphia, Pa., Bag making machine and fountain pen.

PAUL E. JOHNSON—Chicago, Therapeutic lamp.

J. B. JACKSON—Mass., trolley wheel also heating and lighting devices.

W. D. HARPER—Ohio, system for making fertalizer out of garbage.

H. JULIAN—Canada, Parachute for airplanes.

MOSES AMOS—Ga., box stamping device.

ARTHUR L. MacBETH, Baltimore—Daylight moving picture machine.

J. SMART—Indianapolis—Locomotive connecting rod gear device.

CHARLES V. RICHEY—Telephone registration machine

B. F. BRYANT—Florida, new type steam engine.

HENRY BLAIR—Maryland. Corn harvester.

BENJAMIN A. CRENSHAW—Chicago, Ill., December 1931, Direction Signal for Automobiles.

BENJAMIN BANNEKER—America's first striking clock also invented an Almanac.

F. DOUGLAS WARNER—N. Y., airplane self starter.

CLAUDE E. HARVARD—Automatic gauging machine. Used in Ford auto plants.

HENRY CRAMER—N. Y., steam traps.

WILLIAM SOLDER—Boston, Cooking stove and hot water heater.

WALTER CUNNINGHAM—Pa., device for tapping bolts.

ALICE H. PARKER—N. J., heating furnace.

JOSEPH H. DICKINSON—Automatic piano player.

MARY J. REYNOLDS—Mo., Hoist for moving packages from 2nd story windows.

SOLMON HARPER—N. Y., Electric signal system for trains.

FRANK J. FERRELL—Valves for steam engines.

HERBERT G. WILLIAMS—Ohio, device for using engine exhaust gas twice.

JAMES MOORE—Chicago, Bladder Drainer. Copyright No. 18232.

CHAS J. PERRY—Chicago, Ill., Gas manifold and ignition combination.

CHAS. J. PERRY—Chicago, Ill. Patent applied for Hydro-Carbon burner attachment for locomotive fire box.

E. BURDEN—Cleveland, Ohio, Reversed Fingers, 3 in 1 Glove, 2 Patents issued. Nov. 16th, 1920—March 8th, 1927, June 4th, 1929, and March 17th, 1931.

ELBERT R. ROBINSON—Chicago, Ill. 1897, Casting for Composite Wheels and Other Castings.

ELBERT R. ROBINSON—Chicago, Ill. March 1898, Trolley Wheel.

ELBERT R. ROBINSON—Chicago, Ill. September 1907, Railway Switch.

ELBERT R. ROBINSON—Chicago, Ill. May 1908, Street Car Rail.

ELBERT R. ROBINSON—Chicago, Ill. May 1908, Cast Iron Axle.

ELBERT R. ROBINSON—Chicago, Ill. September 1914, Pneumatic Tire for Motor Vehicle.

A FEW OF OUR CHAMPIONS

JACK JOHNSON—Heavyweight champion of the world.

SAM LANGFORD—The greatest pugalist of his weight.

TIGER FLOWERS — Middleweight champion of the world.

JACK THOMPSON — Welterweight Champion of the world.

BATTLING SIKI—Light heavyweight champion of the world.

PANAMA AL BROWN — Bantamweight champion of Europe.

JOHN HENRY LEWIS—Light heavyweight champion of the world.

HENRY ARMSTRONG—Feather-light and welterweight champion of the world, 1938.

SATCHELL PAGE—Said to be the world's greatest baseball pitcher. Beat Dizzy Dean in his prime.

JOHN BROOKS DENBY—Champion Negro golfer.

W .C. HANDY—Song composer, author of St. Louis Blues.

HAROLD WHEELER—Atlanta, Ga., won 13th National Open Golf Championship, Chicago, 1938.

MRS. MEL MOYE—Of Atlanta, Ga., won 9th Woman's National Golf Title 1938.

RENE MARAN—Wrote book called "Batouala" in 1921, won Prix Goncourt for best French novel.

LEONARD TYNER—Marbel Shooting Champion of the world.

ARTHUR PRINCE—Hoop Rolling Champion.

LEWIS ARMSTRONG—America's greatest cornetist.

CLARENCE CAMERON WHITE—Violinist of national renown.

DUKE ELLINGTON—Band leader and record song composer.

MANCY CAMPBELL—Greatest trap drummer of his time.

ETHEL WATERS—Stage and screen star, Blues singing champion.

BILL ROBINSON—Over 50 years old, still champion tap dancer.

BERT A. WILLIAMS—Premier comedian of America and Europe.

ROLAND HAYES—Greatest lyric tenor singer.

JOSEPH RAGLAN—Champion brick layer — laid 3,472 bricks per hour.

ISAAC MURPHY—World's greatest jockey, won Kentucky Derby three times.

DUKE SLATER — University of Iowa, Iowa's greatest tackle.

SAMUEL WINNINGHAM—Watermelon King of Chicago, Ills.

THOMAS FULLER—A Virginia slave, world's fastest calculator.

TYDIA PICKETT—Runner of international renown—in Olympics 1936 in Germany.

GRANVILLE T. WOODS—Great electrical inventor has record of over 300 patented inventions.

GEORGE W. CARVER — World's greatest agricultural chemist, Tuskegee, Alabama.

MARCUS GARVEY—Founder of U. N. I. A., greatest organizer of his time.

DR. DAN WILLIAMS—Chicago, first surgeon to successfully stitch the human heart.

TENTH U. S. CAVALRY—Greatest all around unit of the United States Army.

COLONEL CHARLES YOUNG—Considered to be the best, and the most mistreated U. S. soldier.

THOMAS BETHUNE (Blind Tom)—The world's greatest blind pianist.

CORTEZ W. PETERS — Fastest typist in the world. Average 133 words a minute, for a solid hour.

CHEVALIER DE ST. GEORGES—France's champion Swordsman, Skater, Bare-back Rider, Poet and Violinist.

WILLIE (SUICIDE) JONES—Set parachute jump record of 29,400 feet, Chicago, August 28th, 1938.

ROSCOE C. SIMMONS—America's foremost political campaign orator.

WILLA B. BROWN—Fearless licensed woman air pilot of Chicago.

TWENTY-FOURTH U. S. INFANTRY—Crack unit of the United State Army.

EDWIN O. GOURDIN—Harvard University winner of National Pentathlon, 1921.

BINGA DESMOND—Champion runner of the world.

RALPH METCALF—Champion runner of the world — broke or equalled all sprint records.

EDDIE TOLAN—World's champion runner, University of Michigan.

MAJOR TAYLOR—World's champion cycalist about 1899.

JESSE OWENS—Fastest runner that ever lived, holder of three different titles, 1938.

DAVE ALBRITTON—Co-holder of high jump record, Ohio State, 1937.

MELVIN WALKER—Great star of Ohio State 1937.

ED BURKE—Athletic champion of Marquette.

BILL WATSON—University of Michigan, great field star.

GIL GRUTER—Athletic star, University of Colorado.

EULACE PEACOCK—Champion runner, Temple University.

THOMAS NELSON—Fresno, California, track and field champion.

DONALD DUNN—of Pittsburgh, Kansas, unexcelled on track and field.

JOSHUA WILLIAMSON — XAVIER University, New Orleans, La.

WILBER MILLER—Compton, California, great athlete.

JOHNNIE WOODRUFF—University of Pittsburgh, Pa., world's champion runner.

JAMES HERBERT—Champion of New York University.

JIM SMITH—Indiana University track and field star.

ARCHIE WILLIAMS—University of California Athletic star.

WOODROW STRODE—U.C.L.A., great performer track star.

GEORGE ROBERTSON—Drake Uuiversity, outstanding 1937 track star.

MACK ROBINSON—University of Oregon, champion on track and field.

JEROME HOLLAND—Football star Cornell University.

HOMER HARRIS—University of Iowa, foot ball star.

OZZIE SIMMONS—University of Iowa, great half back.

HORACE BELL—University of Minnesota, unexcelled all-around athlete.

FRANK KELKER—Western Reserve football star.

KENNY WASHINGTON—U.C.L.A.—Best of the eleven.

BERNARD JEFFERSON—Northwestern football wizard.

DON HINTON—Northwestern foot ball star.

FRIZT POLLARD, SR.—Brown University, outstanding football star.

FRITZ POLLARD, JR.—Famous like his father, North Dakota.

INK WILLIAMS—Brown University had no superior in football.

CORNELIUS JOHNSON—Ohio State, 1937 co-holder of world's high jump record.

TOM MULINEAUX—First American heavyweight champion, a champion while in slavery.

GEORGE DIXON—Featherweight champion of the world.

PETER JACKSON—Heavyweight, fought 61 round draw with James J. Corbett.

JOE WALCOTT—Welterweight champion of the world.

JOE GANS—Lightweight champion of the world.

JAMES LEE—Negro jockey, rode 6 straight winners in one day at Churchill Downs, 1907.

GUSTAVE SAVAGE—New York City, produced the "Harp", most attractive statue at New York World's Fair, 1939.

WM. STILL—race composer, wrote the theme song for New York Worlds Fair.

CLIFFORD BLOUNT—Chicago's armless wonder business man, types 40 words a minute and can fully dress himself in ten minutes.

A LESSON IN BLACK

BLACK—Black was the color of the angels of early Ethiopians.

BLACK—Ethiopians painted their devils white.

BLACK—Madonna was the mother of Jesus Christ.

BLACK—Was the color of the ancient Jews.

BLACK—Is the name of one of the managers of Joe Louis.

BLACK—Burn, was the name of the chief trainer of Joe Louis.

BLACK—Cities have no major crimes and some have no jails.

BLACK—Is the color of the most attractive rose developed in Germany.

BLACK—People were found in Asia before they were found in Africa.

BLACK—Side of a Halibut Fish has 2 eyes, white side has no eyes.

BLACK—Belt has produced no lynchers or kidnapers.

BLACK—Paint is more fadeless than any other color of paint.

BLACK—People are not inferior to other races of humanity.

BLACK—Animals are not discriminated against by white animals.

BLACK—Peoples worst enemies are among themselves.

BLACK—Blood is the strongest blood in the world—one drop makes you whole.

BLACK—Oil is refined for a thousand different uses.

BLACK—Was the color of Jesus Christ, if he was an original Jew.

BLACK—Ink is the most fadeless writing fluid.

BLACK—Angels are being painted in the best black churches.

BLACK—FEET Indians are very friendly to black people.

BLACK—Is a color that only ignorant poor people abhor.

BLACK—Was not the color of America's first slaves.

BLACK—Was the color of "Buddha" the god of India.

BLACK—Legion of 1000 saved the French and American troops at Savannah.

BLACK—Is the color of "Fuhi" the Chinese god.

BLACK—Soil is the most productive soil on earth.

BLACK—Is the color of "Xaha" the worshipful God of Japan.

BLACK—Is the color of coal, producer of light, heat and power.

BLACK—Is the color of "Quetzalcoatl" the god of Mexico.

BLACK—Dolls are being carried by well trained black children.

BLACK—Women are annoyed by white men after dark.

BLACK—Clouds carry the water that fertilize the fields of grain.

BLACK—People are black, because they are nearest the "Sun" of God.

BLACK—Sheep are found in some of the best white families.

BLACK—And darker races outnumber whites four to one.

BLACKS—Number 430,000,000 of the 500,000,000 British Empire.

BLACKS—Number 125,000,000 of the 170,000,000 French Empire.

BLACKS—In Africa outnumber whites sixty to one.

BLACKS—In the Congo outnumber whites a hundred to one.

BLACK—And Brown are the 320,000,000 people of India.

BLACK—Was Cush who founded Ethiopia about 6280 B. C.

BLACK—Was Nimród, son of Cush and founder of Assyrian Empire.

BLACK—Women's affections was one of the losses of southern slavery.

BLACK—Ethiopia has its coptic religion and its Amharic language.

BLACK—Woman's burden, carrying unwanted bastard child of her white master.

BLACK—Was not the color of Giteau, who killed President Garfield.

46

BLACK—Was not the color of Booth, who assasinated President Lincoln.

BLACK—Was not the color of Czologsz, who murdered President McKinley.

BLACK—Was not the color of Zangara, who shot at President Roosevelt and killed Mayor Cermack.

BLACK—Was not the color of Bruno Hauptmann and dozens of other kidnapers.

BLACK—Are the soldiers who fight for the American flag in time of war and are mistreated in all the 48 states in time of peace.

BLACK—Native Africans never had Tuberculosis and Syphilis.

BLACK—"Falashas" is name of Black Jews of Ethiopia.

BLACK—Was Pope Melchiades, who led fight on the Roman Empire.

BLACK—Meat of the Turkey, or any fowl has more calories and proteins than white meat.

BLACK—Domestic servants are so loyal to their employers that kidnappers avoid those homes, and select homes where they find white inside assistance.

BLACK—People are black because they are sun-soaked, and not Cain-cursed.

BLACK—Out is a protection used when white people are slaughtering white people.

BLACK—Pugalist have held all of the 8 championships at some time,—3 have held 5 championships at one time—Joe Louis, heavyweight, John Henry Lewis, light heavyweight, and Henry Armstrong, featherweight, lightweight and welterweight.

BLACK—Markets — so called, are really white markets, where white men are breaking the laws and regulations of white men.

It is no disgrace to be black; a few centuries ago all people were BROWN or BLACK except those who were ravaged by the damnation of disease.

BLACK—Coal when scientifically blended produces articles of many colors, such as Purple, Blue, Red, Green, Amber, Indigo, etc.

GREAT PERSONALITIES OF AFRICAN DESCENT NOW CLAIMED BY WHITE HISTORIANS

JESUS CHRIST—If a Falashas, or an original Jew, He was black.

THE GREAT MADONNA—Was a woman of culture and color.

GEORGE A. P. BRIDGETOWER—Born in Poland of African parents about 1789, greatest violinist of his day.

CHEOPS—Builder of one of seven wonders of the world —the Pyramids, 2,500,000 granite blocks.

CLEOPATRA—Queen of Egypt and most lovely lady of her generation.

QUEEN OF SHEBA—Related to Cush, King Solomon and Hailie Selassie.

SIMON, THE SIREEN—Black man who helped Christ carry his cross up Mt. Calvary.

CRISPUS ATTUCKS—First martyr in the Massacre of Boston Common.

SALEM POOR—The outstanding hero in the Battle of Bunker Hill.

ALEXANDER HAMILTON—Great statesman, secretary of State and member of Continental Congress.

PETER B. S. PINCHBACK—Statesman, once acting governor of Louisiana.

HANNIBAL—Greatest general the world has ever known.

TOSSIANT L'OVERTURE—Greatest soldier and statesman of Haiti.

JO. ANDERSON—Slave of Cyrus McCormick and co-inventor of first mechanical reaper.

HELIODORE C. MORTENOL—Commanded air force of Paris during World War—1914 to 1918.

EUGENE HARVARD—Great inventor of gauging machine at Ford factory, Detroit.

J. E. METZELINGER—Inventor of first automatic shoe lasting machine.

ALEXANDER DUMAS — Great French novelist and thinker.

HARRIET TUBMAN—Orator and anti-slavery underground railroad operator.

RENE MARAN—Prize winning novelist of France.

GRANVILLE T. WOODS—Inventor of telephone receiver and many other great inventions.

ALEXANDER PUSHKIN—Russia's celebrated black poet.

RALPH METCALFE—Champion runner, broke or equalled standard sprint records.

MATTHEW HENSON—Only living man who went to North Pole with Commodore Perry.

GEORGE DIXON—Greatest pugilist of his time, featherweight champion of the world.

PAUL E. JOHNSON—Inventor of therapeautic lamps.

SOLOMON—Wise man, was the wisest of the wise.

BEETHOVEN—Greatest musical composer of his age.

TIPPOO TIB—First great African explorer.

IMHOTEP—Black Egyptian, discovered circulation of blood 5,000 years before Dr. Harvey's announcement in Europe.

JEAN BAPTIST POINT DeSAIBLE—First settler in Chicago, 1779.

PETRO ALONZO—Navigator on ship with Christopher Columbus in discovery of America.

AUGUSTUS JACKSON, of Philadelphia—Credited with discovery of ice cream making process.

CHARLES W. CHESTNUT—Cleveland, Ohio, author of national renown.

ESOP—Ethiopian, once a slave, world's greatest moralist.

GENERAL BENJAMIN F. BUTLER—1818-1893, lawyer politician and civil war general, hero at the battle of New Orleans. He was a mulatto, and the son of a negro barber, see book on Gen. Butler, in New Orleans, by James Parton.

JULIUS CAESAR—Roman general, statesman and historian.

SOME FINE WHITE FRIENDS

ARMSTRONG, General S. C.—He and his wife took great interest in Booker T. Washington.

BROWN, JOHN—Abolutionist from Kansas gave his life to help free black slaves.

BAKER, RAY STANNARD—Writer of note always fair on the race question.

BEECHER, HENRY WARD—Great preacher and friendly to oppressed black people.

CHANNING, WILLIAM E.—Author of note and anti-slavery agitator.

DRESSLER, MARIE—Hollywood actress, bequeathed $50,000 to Mrs. Cox, her Negro maid.

DEBS, EUGENE—Socialist and labor orator. Great friend of the colored race.

DARROW, CLARENCE—Great criminal lawyer, hater of capital punishment and defender of human rights.

EISENHOWER, U. S. GENERAL DWIGHT—Unprejudiced as a civilian and as a soldier.

FORAKER, B.—Ohio Senator who championed the rights of colored soldiers charged with rioting.

FORD, HENRY—Auto manufacturer, gives positions to thousands of Negroes.

FISH, CONGRESSMAN HAMILTON—Requested the command of Negro troops in the 2nd as in the first World War.

FISK, GENERAL CLINTON B.—Ideal personality after whom Fisk University of Nashville, Tenn. was named.

GARRISON, WILLIAM LLOYD—Great orator and enemy to southern slavery.

HUDSON, C. E.—Telegrapher, Banker, The best employer this writer ever had.

HERFORD, AL—Manager of Champion Joe Gans.

INGERSOLL, ROBERT G.—Said "Every time I meet a Negro I feel like getting on my knees to ask him pardon for crimes my race has inflicted on his."

JOLSON, AL—Hollywood actor—has given assistance to many struggling Negroes.

KITSELMAN, BROTHERS—Of Indiana, friends of Amanda Smith, the great Negro Evangelist.

KNOX, FRANK—Chicago newspaper publisher, usually fair on race matters until he became secretary of the Navy in 1940.

LINCOLN, ABRAHAM—Signor of Emancipation Proclamation, 1863.

LOVEJOY, ELIJAH—Abolutionist, lost his life in the cause of Negro freedom.

LA GUARDIA, F.—Mayor of New York City, fair to Negroes when picketing stores for jobs.

McDOWELL, MARY—Chicago Social Worker, unbiased and unprejudiced.

MUNGER, LOUIS D.—Of Indiana found and developed Major Taylor World's Champion Cycalist.

NEW YORK CITY under Mayor Fiorello LaGuardia — Negro given fullest rights of freedom of speech.

OVINGTON, MARY WHITE—Lecturer, writer and defender of human rights.

OBERLIN, JOHN FREDRICK—Oberlin College, one of first to accept Negro students.

PHILLIPS, WENDELL—Abolutionist and hater of chattel slavery.

PULLMAN, GEORGE—Designer of the Pullman Car— said to have requested "perpetual employment of Negro porters."

QUEENSTOWN, IRELAND—Never had traffic in slavery.

ROOSEVELT, THEODORE—26th President, always fair on matters of race.

ROSENWALD, JULIUS—Jewish philanthropist, very generous to Negro institutions.

ROOSEVELT, FRANKLIN D.—President of the U. S. He and wife unbiased to Negroes.

SUMNER, CHARLES—A fearless champion of the rights of Negro slaves.

STONE, LUCY—Anti-slavery agitator and orator.

STALIN, JOSIF—Premier of Russia, where black and white have absolute equality.

SPINGARN, JOEL E.—Gives a medal annualy to a Negro for the most outstanding achievement.

TAGGART, THOMAS—Of French Lick Springs, employer of many race men and women.

T. A. D.—The late cartoonist and writer. Very fair to Negro pugilists and athletes.

THOMPSON, WILLIAM HALE—Former Mayor of Chicago, set precedence in the employment of Negroes.

UNTERMEYER, S.—Great lawyer fair on the question of race.

VOLNEY, COUNT—Speaks well of black people in his book "Ruins of Empires."

VILLARD, OSWALD GARRISON—Writer and orator, a believer in human rights.

VILAS, W. F.—Wisconsin Senator gave 10 scholarships to Negro students.

WILBERFORCE WILLIAMS—Helped abolish slavery in England.

WALGREEN DRUG STORES—Set a precedent in giving responsible positions to Negro in their Chicago drug stores.

XENIANS—Of Xenia, Ohio house many of the students of Wilberforce University.

YANKEES—Of New England, display a splendid spirit toward Negroes.

YUCATANS—Friendly Mexicans, hospitable to Afro-Americans.

ZIONISTS, JEWS—Generally fair to minority groups.

ZEIGFELD, FLO—Great showman who once starred Bert A. Williams.

DR. JOHN HAYNES HOLMES — N. Y. City, Peoples Church.

DR. PRESTON BRADLEY—Peoples Church, Chicago, Ill.

PEARL BUCK—Writer and friend of all mankind.

GREAT BLACK PEOPLE IN THE HOLY BIBLE

The TRIBE OF JUDAH was a tribe of BLACK PEOPLE
and JESUS CHRIST came from that tribe. Gen. 49:10,
Heb. 7:14, and Rev. 5:5.

HAM was a BLACK MAN and CANAAN was the son of
Ham, Gen. 10:6.

JUDAH had five children and all males, 1st Chron. 2:4.
Three by his first wife and two by his second and both
of his wives were Canaanite women, 1st Chron. 2:3-4.

TAMAR, Judah's second wife, bore him two sons whose
names were Pharez and Zerah, 1st Chron. 2:4.

The name of PHARES appears in the geneology of Jesus
Christ, Matt. 1:3.

The APOSTLE PAUL declared "OUR LORD" sprang out
of JUDAH, Heb. 7:14.

ABRAHAM, the father of the Jews, was one of the first to
marry a BLACK WOMAN, Gen. 25:1.

MOSES, the great Hebrew law-maker and law giver, married BLACK WOMEN also. Gen. 46: 10, 1st Chron. 2:3,
Gen. 41:45.

SIMEON and BARNABAS were BLACK MEN who
taught and preached with the apostles of their day, Acts
13:1.

JESUS was born of the VIRGIN MARY, and she was of
the Tribe of JUDAH and the Tribe of JESUS, Gen. 49:-
10, Heb. 7:14, Rev. 5:5.

SAINT PAUL says JESUS was the seed of DAVID ac-
cording to the flesh, and David is the tenth person from
Judah in the geneology of Jesus Christ, Matt. 1:3-4-5-6.
And David's great-great-grandfather, BOOZ, was born
of the woman RACHAB. She was descendant of HAM
Matt. 1:5.

Therefore, DAVID, whom GOD chose to lead His people,
was also a BLACK MAN by blood.

SOLOMON, the world's most wisdomatic man and the son
of DAVID, told the daughters of Jerusalem "I am black,
but comely." Songs of Solomon 1:5-6.

The BLACK JEWS were Royal Jews and SOLOMON was a Royal Jew.

He constructed the most magnificent Royal Temple ever built on earth.

And SOLOMON'S guest of honor, after the dedication of the temple, was the beautiful BLACK QUEEN OF SHEBA, 1st Kings, 10:1.

One of the queen's ancestors was named SHEBA and SHEBA was the grandchild of KETURAH, the ETHIOPIAN woman, who was ABRAHAM'S second wife, Gen. 25:1-2-3.

Thus we find the QUEEN OF SHEBA, SOLOMON, CUSH, ABRAHÁM, DAVID, HAM and JESUS CHRIST were all related by the Hamitic blood of the great BLACK RACE.

Moses Must Have Been Black

God commanded MOSES to put his hand into his bosom, he obeyed, and when he took it out, behold, it was white as snow.

Then God commanded MOSES to put his hand back into his bosom, he obeyed, and then he pulled his hand out and behold, it was turned as his OTHER FLESH, Ex. 4:6-7.

How Solomon Became Black

SOLOMON said he was black because the SUN had look-upon him, Songs of Solomon, 1:6.

THE WHITE MAN IN THE HOLY BIBLE

The only place in the Holy Bible where I find mention of a WHITE MAN is where he became WHITE by disease. "And he went out from his presence a leper as WHITE as snow." 2nd Kings 5:27.

REV. ROSS D. BROWN.

SOURCES OF AUTHORITY

Names of athletic champions obtained from current World Almanac and National Boxing Record.

Information concerning Moors, Egyptians, Africans, and Ethiopians obtained from historic works of J. A. Rogers, of New York City.

Facts about Sears, of Sears and Roebuck, obtained personally from Rev. John W. Sears of Charleston, W. Va.

Political information concerning Pinchback and conditions in the South, given by Ex-Congressman John R. Lynch, and also obtained while traveling in the Southland.

Facts about President John Tyler's daughter, obtained from book entitled "The White Side of a Black Subject."

Many historic facts used in this work are from the Negro Year Books of 1924 and later issues.

Some facts of the black people in religion were obtained from Count Volney's "Ruins of Empires" of the 17th century.

Other facts of religion and black people are found in the St. James Version—Holy Bible.

Facts about Alexander Hamilton and his nationality may be found in any good work on the life of Hamilton or a book called "The History of the Continental Congress."

Information on patents by Negro Inventors furnished by Henry E. Baker, examiner of patents, Washington, D. C.

Thanks to these great Negro historians: George W. Williams, Carter G. Woodson and my good friend J. A. Rogers. Also to Fredrick H. Robb, the native born African, and the ace of air races, Colonel J. C. Robinson, Eagle of Ethiopia, for information used in this book.

It is reasonable to suppose that thousands of Negroes not listed here have obtained U. S. patents on their inventions, as the patent office keeps no separate list of Negro inventors and their patents— R. D. B.

FIFTEEN MILLION NEGROES ON PARADE

If there was but one person on earth there would be no system, no society, and no sociology.

There would be no enslavement, no ethics, and no etiquette, no styles, no statutes, and no standards, no laws, no leases and no litigations.

But with many persons on earth, laws to govern limitations began to take shape and form, so that each person could receive the proper social consideration.

Today we live in a country that is well settled, eyes and ears are everywhere, and each and every American Negro is passing on parade.

Every woman is watched, every man is marked, and every child is checked. Our crimes are catalogued, and our patriotism is almost forgotten.

Our good traits are quietly recalled, and our mistakes are broadcasted long and loud.

Negroes, however, are only human beings, subject to all the winds and waves of law, love and life. And they are not immune to the mental boll-weevils that cut and crawl into the brain and blood of all the races, royal or ragged, that walk and wing their way around this pole-propped gear driven grain of sand.

The Negro has a long way to go, and before he gets to his goal he will have to stop trying to dress like a Prince on a poor man's pay; he will have to stop buying fine automobiles to decorate the boulevards while he is forced to live in a financial alley.

He will have to stop loafing and swearing on the streets, stop throwing his weekly wages away, stop talking loud and telling his secrets, stop wearing dirty overalls for evening dress, stop letting his children go dingy and dirty, and stop insulting unescorted women.

Our children should not be neglected just because they are Negroes, our women should not be untidy just because they are colored, and no man should be dumb just because he is dark.

We have too many silly citizens who are devoted to dirt, with a weakness for weeds, a prejudice against paint, a fear of flowers, a hatred for home-life, and a grudge against grass.

And when a crime is committed by the worst of us, the consequences must be born by the best of us.

A man should never get so common that he would greet a lady on the street without tipping his hat, never be so ignorant as to think he is indispensable to his boss, and never think he can supplant neatness with negligence.

There is nothing finer in the race than a comely modest woman, a cute immaculate well-mannered baby, and a man who is educated, earnest and honest.

Some day we will learn that vegetables are as delicious as pigs-feet, that fruits are as good as barbecue, and that cereals are as tasty as sorghum.

We are not wanted in white neighborhoods, not always because of race, but often because of risk, not always because we were slaves, but often because we are still asleep, not always because of prejudice, but often because we destroy property, not always because of color, but often because of character, not always because we are wanton, but often because we disrespect women.

For over sixty-five years America has been taking mental flashlights, finger-prints, and photographs of moral character, and social conduct, and they are watching every night; they are checking every day the fifteen million Negroes ON PARADE.

— SUPPLEMENT —
WHAT DO YOU KNOW ABOUT NEGRO HISTORY?
THINGS WE SHOULD KNOW

South Carolina sent 8 colored men to the United States Congress. They were Richard H. Cain, Robert C. Delarge, Robert B. Elliott, Thomas H. Miller, George W. Murray, Joseph H. Rainey, A. J. Ransier, and Robert Smalls.

North Carolina sent four Negroes to Congress—H. P. Cheatham, John Hyman, Jas. E. O'Harra, Geo. H. White.

Alabama sent three race men to Congress—Jeremiah Haralson, James T. Rapier, and Benj. S. Turner. Louisiana sent two Afro-Americans to Congress—J. H. Menard and Charles E. Nash.

Virginia sent one—John M. Langston.

Georgia sent one—Jefferson Long.

Mississippi sent one—John R. Lynch.

Florida sent one—Josiah T. Walls; Illinois sent three —Oscar DePriest, Arthur W. Mitchell and Wm. L. Dawson.

Mississippi sent two colored men to the Senate: they were Hiram R. Revels and Blanche K. Bruce.

Girard College, located in Philadelphia, Pa., was founded by Stephen Girard, as per his request, Ministers or Negroes are not allowed to attend or visit this institution.

Petro Alonzo, a black man, piloted the Nina and made the charts and maps to guide Columbus across the ocean in discovery of America.

Crispus Attucks, a Negro, was the first American soldier to shed his blood in the American revolution at the massacre on Boston Common.

Jean Baptist Point DeSaible, a Santo Dominican Negro, was the first civilized settler in the place now called Chicago, Illinois.

Thomas Greene Bethune, "Blind Tom," was the world's most famous blind musician.

Isaac Murphy, a Negro with an Irish name, was a great jockey. He won the Kentucky Derby in 1884, 1890 and 1891. In 55 years of racing, from 1875 to 1929, the only jockey who won the Kentucky Derby three times was Isaac Murphy.

Granville T. Woods, a Negro, patented a receiver for the Bell Telephone.

"Old Master," the late Joe Gans, won his title from Frank Erne, and is credited with being the only pugilist who ever won a championship with one blow.

Toussaint L'overture was a sable soldier, statesman, and Liberator, and was said to be the greatest general of his day.

James Parker, a Negro, knocked Czologosz down when he shot President McKinley at the Buffalo Exposition.

A black slave by the name of Jo Anderson worked with Cyrus Hall McCormick, and was the co-inventor of the McCormick reaper. Slaves could invent but they could not procure patents as they were not citizens. But this slave was the inventor of the world's first mechanical reaper.

John Tyler, tenth president of the United States, sold his daughter into slavery because she eloped to Canada and tried to marry a Negro slave.

Matthew A. Henson, an Afro-American, went to the North Pole with Perry and planted the Stars and Stripes at the North Pole.

Negro pugilists have held many divisional world championships: Jack Johnson, heavyweight; Tiger Flowers, middleweight; Joe Walcott, welterweight; Jack Thompson, twice welterweight champion; Joe Gans, lightweight; George Dixon, featherweight, and Al Brown, bantamweight champion. Many other good fighters, such as Peter Jackson, Sam Langford and Kid Chocolate were better than some champions.

Elijah McCoy invented the best lubricator of his day.

Benjamin Banneker, Negro astronomer, invented America's first striking clock and the first almanac.

A colored woman named Jenkins was the inventor of Aunt Jemima's pancake flour.

Negro mountain about two thousand feet high is in the state of Maryland on highway 40, about 90 miles east of Wheeling, West Va.

On February 25th, 1938, Henry Armstrong, Featherweight Champion of the world knocked out Everett Rightmire in Chicago in the 3rd round.

THINGS THEY DON'T WANT US TO KNOW

Negro slaves were brought to America in 1619, and on July 4th, 1776 they had been enslaved for 157 years, and remained in slavery 87 years after Independence Day, and were not emancipated until 1863. Therefore the Negro has no right to celebrate on July 4th.

William Turner was lynched in Georgia, May 1918. His wife, Mary Turner, was strung up by the heels, her abdomen was ripped open with a long butcher knife and her eight month old baby dropped out of her womb.

A cruel southern craker crushed it's little head with the heel of his boot.

John Ernest Metzelinger, a Negro, was the inventor of an automatic shoe soling machine. His patents founded the United Shoe Machinery Company. He died at home in Lynn, Mass., in 1889 at the age of 37.

Peter B. S. Pinchback, a Negro, was acting Governor of the State of Louisiana for several months.

The Metropolitan Life Insurance Co., pretends to carry life insurance on Negroes who pay them more than $60,000,-000 per year. A Negro has life Insurance in a company for which he can work. But he only has DEATH Insurance in a company that only pays his death claim after he dies.

The Century of Progress in Chicago, 1933-34, was the only world's fair ever held in a district represented in Washington by a Negro Congressman.

November 12, 1928, Lionel Lichorich of Barbadoes, B. W. I., was the hero of the Steamship Vestries disaster. This West Indian Negro saved the lives of 23 persons single handed.

He was welcomed to the City Hall by the Mayor of New York and sold pieces of his clothing for souvenirs.

Varick street in New York City runs from Clarkson to Canal street. This street has a bank and post office bearing its name. Varick street was named after James Varick, a Negro born about 1750 in Newburg, N. Y.

Rev. James Varick was also the first Bishop of the A. M. E. Zion Church.

His mother and father helped to organize Mother Zion Church, and a relative of his family was once Mayor of New York City.

In 1933 Chicago Italians had 7th Street changed to Balbo Avenue in honor of the great Italian aviator. A few years previous Washington Park Court, on which Chicago Negroes live, was re-named De Saible Court, in honor of Chicago's first settler.

Negroes objected to living on a street named after a Negro, and had the street name changed back to Washington Park Court.

Robert H. Wood, Negro, was once Mayor of Natchez, Mississippi.

Elbert R. Robinson of Chicago was the inventor of a groove street car rail, a welding process, and other inventions.

William Walker, a great Negro jockey, rode the winning horse in the great match race at Churchill Downs, July 4th, 1878, when Ten Brook beat Mollie McCarthy. He also won the Kentucky Derby, riding Baden in 1877.

Ras Desta Demptu dined at the White House with President Franklin D. Roosevelt in 1933. Demptu was the son-in-law of Emperor Haile Selassie of Ethiopia.

After the world's best detectives had tried in vain, William Allen, a New Jersey Negro truck driver, found the dead body of the kidnapped Lindburgh baby.

"The Darkest Africa" exhibit at the World's Fair in Chicago, 1933, exhibited an ex-American sailor multilated by the knives of Africans for having insulted a black African woman. African black men are race patriots — not pimps.

The Prudential Life Insurance Co., that refuses to insure Negroes, has the Rock of Gibralter as it's trade-mark emblem. Surely they do not know that this large rock was discovered by black men, and also named after a black man, long before the birth of Christ.

On July 12th, 1936, in the new Randall Island Stadium, Cornelius Johnson and Dave Albritton, before a crowd of 21,000 people broke the world high jump record with unbelievable twin leaps of six feet, nine and three-fourths inches. Both of these colored boys jumped higher than man had ever jumped before.

Mr. James L. Green . . . . . auto salesman employed by the Drexel Chevrolet Company of Chicago is the only Negro in America holding a membership in the Two Hundred Club.

Lawnside, N. J. — America's oldest Race city, was one hundred years old in 1940.

E. SIMS CAMPBELL, originator of "Cuties" cyndicated cartoons is a Negro.

The merchant ship the S. S. "Marine Eagle" first American Merchant ship built entirely by Negroes and christened by Mrs. Rachel Stevenson, matron of the Sun Ship Building Co., of Chester, Pa., launched May 10th, 1943.

Jan. 1—1861—ISAAC MURPHY was born, Lexington, Ky., great jockey, three times winner of Kentucky Derby.

PETER JACKSON fought a 61-round draw with JAMES J. CORBETT May 21, 1891.

ADELL WHITE of Monahans, Texas, is believed to be the youngest American mother. At 10 years of age, she gave birth to an 8 pound, 8 ounce baby daughter. January 1st, 1944.

THINGS THEY DON'T TEACH IN SCHOOL

Paul E. Johnson of Chicago, is the inventor and patentee of a therapeutic lamp.

Mr. Johnson also procured patents on physiotherapy equipment, now in use all over the world.

Charles C. Dawson of Chicago, is an artist of the first magnitude. He is said to be the only Negro member of the Art Students League of New York City.

Junius G. Groves of Kansas, was best known as the "Potato King." In one year on his five hundred acre farm he produced one hundred thousand bushels of white potatoes.

He achieved the distinction of growing more potatoes, per hill on an acre than any other Potatoist. Before his death he was said to be worth over $80,000.

"Listen to the Lambs" is one of the greatest songs ever written. It came from the musical soul of one of the world's greatest composers, Nathaniel R. Dett, the matchless musical monarch of Hampton Institute.

The late James Reese Europe was the able leader of the old 15th N. Y. Negro regiment band. His music inspired Negroes to fight for a country in time of war, that would not let them vote for themselves in time of peace.

A number of Negroes have attended West Point Military Academy, at West Point, N. Y.

Henry O. Flipper, John H. Alexander, and Charles Young, were the first graduates. It is said that black students at West Point have been humiliated, and run away by imprintable and indescribable treatment. However, there are about two hundred Negroes at West Point.

And while they are segregated and discriminated against the most of them have a far better knowledge of drilling, and the science of war than the officers from whom they take orders.

The careful findings of Professor Weiner prove beyond a doubt that black men were here long before Columbus arrived.

A black man named ESTEVANICO is said to have traversed the plains of Texas, and Mexico for eight years. He is credited by some historians as having discovered the above mentioned territory, including Arizona.

Sojourner Truth was an anti-slavery orator. She was known by all of the abolitionist speakers, and is said to have visited President Abraham Lincoln in the White House.

The first shot at the Battle of Bunker Hill was fired by a Negro, Peter Salem. This shot caused the death of Major Pitcairn.

Beach Sampson was the real name of "Black Sampson of Brandywine" who took a mowing scythe and cut down the best and bravest men of the British Army.

Meta Vaux Warrick of Massachusetts was the best known race woman Sculptor of her time. She studied abroad and won the unstinted praise of the best European critics.

Mary Howard Jackson of Washington, D. C., was also a Sculptress of great ability, and Edmonia Lewis of New York had the ability to make statutes that moved men to tears.

Mighty Major Taylor was an Indianapolis, Ind. boy. He became the champion cyclist of the world, and raced all over Europe.

He was once a wealthy property owner, in Worcester, Mass. He died penniless in Chicago in 1932, and was buried by James Bowler, an old white racing rival.

The Haitian flag is blue and red. The Liberian flag is red-yellow-blue-white and black. The Ethiopian flag is green-yellow and red. Garvey's U. N. I. A. flag is red-black and green.

This writer does not smoke, However, if I smoked cigarettes I would smoke CAMEL Cigarettes because about two-thirds of the women working in the Reynolds tobacco Co. plant are Negro Women.

On the current issue of paper ten dollar bills, will be found the picture of Alexander Hamilton, a Negro.

In Farmville, Va., there is a Negro church in the heart of the city just opposite the Post Office.

In Raleigh, N. C., in the heart of the city the State House sits opposite a large Negro church.

Rev. JOHN W. SEARS, of Charleston, W. Va., is a distant relative of Gen. Robert E. Lee, and also claims to be a relative of two Negroes—Jessie and Jordan Sears respectively, father and grand father of Mr. Sears of Sears and Roebuck.

In Toledo, Ohio, VAN WERT, Darke County, Ohio and Kittanning, Pa., and a few other cities, some Negroes are so light in color that they cannot be distinguished from white people.

A large electrical company in Chicago, in advertising a certain sun lamp, says: "Get a Sun-Tan and possess a dark ruddy healthy complexion, don't be a pale face."

January 1943 — The newly launched Liberty Ship "BOOKER T. WASHINGTON" and its captain HUGH N. MULZAC returned to America on its successful maiden voyage with its Negro Captain and it's crew of many races.

MISS RUTH WASHINGTON of Philadelphia, Pa. is a versatile Registered Nurse, and a skilled Laboratory Technician. Her fine personality, her worth and workmanship has won her the highest honors in the field of her profession.

THINGS OUR CHILDREN SHOULD KNOW

In Baltimore, Md., Oct. 16th, 1934, I stood with bowed head at the grave of Joe Gans. How strange is it that Gans is buried in Auburn cemetery that fronts on Annapolis Ave. and Annapolis road. While Annapolis does not want Negroes in her military academy, and the Auburn Motor company hires no Negroes to help build her machines. But little Joe Gans was so fair in his fighting career that he would have given a gorilla the bigger club, and a rattle snake the first bite.

White men have never hated more than half of the Negro race.

Thomas Jefferson, once President of the United States, and the Father of the Declaration of Independence was said to have been the father of many mullato children.

In Houston, Texas, in 1917, a white policeman ran a Negro boy into a Negro home. A Negro woman was bathing and protested the invasion. The white policeman arrested and took the naked woman down the street. Corporal Charles W. Baltimore of the 24th Infantry and other Negro soldiers came to the woman's rescue, and were beaten—the Houston riot ensued. 19 policemen were killed, 19 brave soldiers were hanged. Some went to Leavenworth prison for life. But all were fighting for the protection of a Negro woman.

A mixed prize fight is the only place in America where a Negro can whip a white man without running the risk of being lynched.

Augustus Jackson a Philadelphia Negro is said to be the inventor of ice cream.

Patriotic Patrick Henry a signer of the Independence document is credited with being the father of a Negro woman's offspring.

William Hampton, a Negro of Indianapolis, Ind., discovered a process for vulcanizing leather with which to make automobile tires.

Lewis Stewart; a Negro of Los Angeles, Cal., invented a practical re-fillable fuse plug.

William Burns, a Negro, who is said to have won his place during a strike, was a passenger engineer on one of the fastest trains of the Indianapolis division of the Pennsylvania railroad.

Blanch K. Bruce, J. C. Napier, W. L. Lyons and W. T. Vernon were once Registers of the United States Treasury.

The Dionne quintuplets had scarcely been born in Canada when an African woman came forth with sextuplets. She and her babies were doing well at this writing.

Abraham Lincoln issued the Emancipation Proclamation in 1863, and a colored woman, Charlotte Scott of Ohio is credited with being the first contributor to a Lincoln monument.

After more than twelve thousand books had been written by white authors on the life of Lincoln, William E. Lilly, a Chicago attorney was the first Negro to write a standard size book on the life of Lincoln. In 1932 he wrote a book entitled: "Let My People Go."

Isaac Murphy, Alonzo Clayton, Monk Overton, Soup Perkins, Felix Carr, Rollie Colston, Andy Hamilton Winkfield, and Willie Simms were Negroes and the greatest jockeys that ever lived.

But today Negro jockeys are not permitted to ride in the Kentucky Derby, Monkey jockys are permitted to ride dogs and ponies on many of the great race tracks of America.

A Chicago Negro, Ralph Metcalfe, the world's greatest runner in 1935 has broken or equalled every standard sprinting record in the world.

August 25, 1935 — This writer spoke with A. Philip Randolph at the first meeting of the Brotherhood of Sleeping Car Porters, New York City.

President Franklin D. Roosevelt had luncheon with a Negro, PRESIDENT EDWIN BARCLAY in Monrovia, Liberia, January 1943.

THINGS THE PREJUDICED PRESS WON'T PRINT

The great Pyramids. The greatest of the seven wonders of the world was designed by Cheops, a brilliant black man. This great structure contains two million and five hundred thousand blocks of time tested gray granite. Each block weighs two and a half tons, and covers more than a dozen acres of sun swept land. It took one hundred thousand black men thirty years to build this four hundred and fifty foot world wonder that has mystified engineering science since its completion in 3730 B. C.

John Brown the great abolitionist had to kill a free Negro traitor before he started to fight to free the slaves. Brown was later hanged with a rope furnished by the State of Kentucky.

William B. Purvis of Philadelphia secured many patents on machinery for making paper bags. He was a Negro.

Jack Johnson was the only heavyweight to win a world's championship without nose bleed, a black eye, broken hands, mussed hair, or a cauliflower ear, and he met no man clever enough to avoid his left hand block, or his right hand uppercut.

In 1934 thousands of Germans voted in America, then went to Germany where they voted in the Saar election. While millions of patriotic Negroes were barred from voting in the United States.

There is said to have been two Popes of the Roman Catholic Church who were of African origin. Their names were Victoria and Merchades.

In 1905 Ross D. Brown invented and secured three United States patents on an automatic glass gathering machine. This machine was used at Corning, N. Y., at the Skillen Goodin glass factory, in Yorktown, Ind., and also at the Hemingray glass factory in Munice, Ind.

Joe Walcott, once welterweight boxing champion of the world, was the only pugilist who could accurately name the round in which he would knock out his opponent.

The editors of the "Chicago Whip," Joe Bibb and A. C. MacNeal, popularized the slogan: "Don't spend your money where you cannot work."

In the winter of 1929, Calvin Saunders picketed a Consumers' grocery store single-handed. Saunders was arrested several times.

A man named Euhul was the second person to take up the single-handed picketing. Then the "Chicago Whip" officially took up the management of the fight against the unfair policy of the F. W. Woolworth five and ten cent stores.

Sufi Abdul Hamid was one of the first men in the great outdoor speaking campaign. Names of the many pickets and contributors are not known. But many of the infamous traitors and trouble makers will never be forgotten.

George Holt, Luegemes Bratton, Catherine Tooley, David Smith, Rebecca J. Holt, James Hale Porter and Qudelious Hardy were speaking under the direction of this writer.

Big Bill Tate handled the pickets in this campaign that started June 7th and ended Oct. 9th, 1930.

Today four Woolworth stores and practically all other stores in Chicago's black belt give employment to Negro clerks.

Thanks to Attorney Herman E. Moore and Wendell E. Green who fought our cases in court.

Thanks to Rev. J. C. Austin and other ministers who enthusiastically supported our cause. And success to the girls and boys many of whom have expressed no thanks for the positions they hold.

In Raleigh, N. C., Negroes not only have a bank, but they also have a bus line of their own, and white people who ride those busses are given no special seats.

A halibut fish has a white side and a black side. On the white side of the head, there are no eyes, on the black side there are two eyes.

JOSEPH RAGLAN of East St. Louis, Illinois, is the champion brick layer, has laid 3,472 bricks an hour, or almost 58 per minute.

There was a greater demonstration of good sportsmanship at the Lewis-Braddock fight than is usually found among white people in the churches in America.

The one country that does not pretend to believe in the Fatherhood of God, is doing more than any other country to practice the brotherhood of man.

ROBERT RIPLEY says: "They had skyscrapers in North Africa, Anemiter near Morocco before they were built in New York City."

In 1942—HOWARD (Skippy) SMITH and EDDIE (Rochester) Anderson, founded the Pacific Parachute Co., in San Diego, Cal. A factory with many races, no discrimination and no color line.

SUPPLEMENT OF HISTORIC EVENTS

APRIL 28, 1941—The U. S. Supreme Court upheld Congressman Arthur W. Mitchell in his case against railroad Jim Crowism.

MARCH 17th, 1941—The City of Philadelphia gave Marion Anderson, the "Noted Negro Singer" the $10,000 Philadelphia award.

OCTOBER 14th, 1941, Seattle, Washington—A. Phillip Randolph, at the 61st A. F. of L. Convention bitterly assailed big wigs of the A. F. of L. for discrimination against Negroes.

FELIX COOPER—Great Cowboy, is a great favorite with the Rodeo fans everywhere.

SEPT. 29th, 1941—JOE LOUIS knocked out Lou Nova in New York. Louis played with Nova for 5 rounds awaiting his much publicized "Yoga Punch," then beat him up so badly in the 6th round that Mike Jacobs junked the half million dollar fight pictures. Explaining that Nova was beaten up so badly that such a picture would injure the fight game.

JULY 7th, 1940—Guessing at the route, FRED RENKE, a Milwaukee Negro, won the 60 mile international outboard marathon race. The boat overturned with the original driver, CHET GUNKLE (white). The Negro righted the boat, bailed out the water, then adjusted his engine and started last. Without a map of the St. Clair river, he out-ran all other boats and finished first far in the lead.

OCTOBER 29, 1940—DR. L. K. WILLIAMS, President of the National Baptist Convention, was killed in a plane crash near OLIVET, MICHIGAN.

71

SUPPLEMENT OF HISTORIC EVENTS

The "March on Washington" organization, headed by A. Phillip Randolph, planned its march for July 1st, 1941. The march was postponed when President Roosevelt sent out an executive order against discrimination in the defense industries of America.

DETROIT, MICHIGAN, OCTOBER 8, 1941

In a drug store window on Hastings street, I saw and counted 44 different kinds of books on dreams, good luck, and numbers. I also counted 30 different kinds of lucky charms, incense and gupher dust. Also I saw several kinds of push button switch blade knives, but nothing on Negro history, sociology, mechanics or philosophy.

DORIE MILLER
THE UNSUNG HERO OF PEARL HARBOR

On Dec. 7th, 1941 when a Japanese torpedo struck the U. S. battleship Arizona in Pearl Harbor, a brave Negro mess attendant, disregarded the fact that he, nor men of his race were permitted to train or practice as gunners on U. S. war ships, manned a machine gun on the bridge of the Arizona and heroically fired it until his ammunition was exhausted.

THE RETURN OF HALLIE SALASSIE

May 6th, 1941, after the rulers of the majority of the European countries had planned and plotted the subjugation and overthrow of Ethiopia.

Hallie Selassie, King of Kings, Conquering lion of the tribe of Judah, the mighty Monarch who descended from the Queen of Sheba and King Solomon went back to his solid Throne of Gold.

While many of the rulers who had planned his downfall, were either dethroned, exiled or executed in their own conquered countries.

A GAMBLER WITH COMMON SENSE

On Feb. 12th, 1940, Benjamin and Pearl Mason with their two children of Philadelphia, Pa. witnessed the ground breaking of their famous Frances Plaza Apartments. An $85,000.00 Housing development.

The Mason family once long on relief, rose from rags to riches, by the winning of a $150,000 sweepstakes prize.

Instead of throwing his wealth away, on fine cars, worthless women, gamblers and superstition dust, he put his money into a practical development to help the poor people of his rent-ridden race.

THE AFRICAN FOOT SLAPPER

Sept. 1st 1941, Robert Ripley cartooned an African bushman, whose feet are faster than an opponents hands. Standing on one foot, and slapping with the other, he slapped his opponent 2400 times before (slapping him out) knocking him out.

JOHNNY BORICAN

July 4th 1940, Brigeton, N. J. Competing for the Asbury Park, N.J.A.C. Johnny Borican became the new A.A.U. Decathlon champion. Borican, the greatest mud runner of his time, broke all records, and won by 5,892 points. He died, Dec. 22, 1942.

GENTLEMAN JOE LOUIS

Jan. 14th, 1942. There are millions of people, of all races, young and old in America and throughout the civilized world who do not know the titles and names of the Mayors of their Cities, Governors of their states, Congressmen and Senators of their respective districts. Many of them do not know and may not care to know the names of the highest ranking figures of their communities. But most all of them know that JOE LOUIS, a NEGRO, is the heavyweight boxing champion of the world.

Joe Louis is quiet and unassuming, modest and manly. From the cotton fields in Alabama where he was born on

May 13th, 1914, to the packed grand stands, from coast to coast, he has lived clean, thought straight, and punched hard. If you don't believe it, ask Max Schmeling, for in their second fight, Louis hit Schmeling so hard in front, that he broke his backbone behind.

Joe Louis was the first Afro-American, to win the heavyweight championship in America. Joe never picked his opponents, as John L. Sullivan did, he never fought a sick man as was the case when James J. Corbett fought that memorable 61 round draw with Peter Jackson. And he never drew the color line like James J. Jeffries and Jack Dempsey. His marvelous, unspotted record, proves him to be, by far, the greatest heavyweight champion the world has ever known.

Joe Louis never picked his opponents. He did not care about their height, reach, weight, or color. He never argued about rounds, rules, referees, rings or regulations, bandages, gloves, tape or timekeepers. He never back-peddeled, fouled or fiddled. He never rabbit-punched, or disobeyed the rigid rules of the royal game. But all the foul tricks that he refrained from doing to others, without complaint, he often had them done to him.

Joe Louis started boxing as an amateur in 1934. To date he has engaged in 56 bouts in eight years. He has been knocked out once, won 7 decisions, and has 48 knock-out victories to his credit.

Joe Louis won his heavyweight championship from James J. Braddock June 22nd, 1937 in Chicago, Illinois. He has to date successfully defended his title twenty times in less than five years. Almost three times as often as any other heavyweight champion.

On Jan. 9th, 1942, he did something no other athletic champion has ever done. He risked his million dollar title, and fought Buddie Bear for nothing—giving all his earnings (nearly a hundred thousand dollars) to the Navy fund. He knocked out Buddie Bear in two minutes, and fifty-six seconds of the first round, and on Jan. 14th, 1942, Joe temporarily at least, laid aside his untarnished crown, and volunteered into the United States army, at Camp Upton, N.

Y. and became a private soldier at about $21.00 per month. On Jan. 21st, of the same year, Joe Louis was special guest at the annual New York boxing writers association dinner.

Joe was awarded the Edward J. Neil memorial plaque, for having done the most for boxing in 1941, and the Ring Magaine Trophy for being the most outstanding boxer of the year. Three Ex-heavyweight champions were photographed with Louis. Gene Tunney, Jack Dempsey and James J. Braddock. Former Mayor of New York—Jimmie Walker looked on and said, Joe you are a great American, a great Negro—you have placed a red rose on Abraham Lincoln's grave.

LEROY SATCHELL PAIGE

Satchell Paige is the world's greatest baseball pitcher. He can do as much with a baseball as George W. Carver has done with the peanut. He can throw all kinds of balls, but he specializes with his famous fast ball.

He has three different fast balls, his fast ball, his-faster ball and his-fastest ball.

He can throw a ball so fast that the batter can't hit it, the catcher doesn't want it and the umpire can't call it.

He walks like Bert Williams, looks like Stepin Fetchet and throws a furious fast ball that travels faster than the down-hill speed of the Broadway Limited. He throws a ball so wizardly fast that it doesn't even whistle, it hasn't got time.

AMERICA

The song "America" — "My Country Tis of Thee, Sweet Land of Liberty", was written by Samuel Francis Smith in the year of 1833 and sung in America for thirty years before America emancipated her four million Black Slaves.

NEGRO BLOOD

George S. Schuyler in his book on "Racial intermarriage in the United States"—says page 7 and 8, Dr. Plecker, Major Cox, and John Powell in their zeal to get a racial integrity law passed in Virginia, made a thorough investigation into the geanologies in that state, and finally announced the sad news that there were no Indians in Virginia, and few on the atlantic coast without Negro ancentry, and had not been for a century.

This blasted the bragging of many of the first families of Virginia who had long boasted of their Indian forbears and claimed descent from the Immortal Pocahontas.

The Richmond News Leader created a stir by saying, that among those living, and dead, who would be classed as Negroes if the bill became a law were—

Two United States Senators
A United States Ambassador to France
Five Generals
Two Presidents of the United States
Two Secretaries of War
Three distinguished southern novelists
Three Governors of Virginia
A speaker of the House of Representatives
Two Bishops
Three Congressmen
One Rear Admiral
Two Judges of the Virginia Supreme Court
And many of the foremost officers of the Confederate army.

Virginia of course is not the only state that would find similar situations if a careful survey were made.

RETRIBUTION

From 600 years B. C. until this present day, millions of men have died in the boomerang of disguised economic warfare to decide which predatory Nation should next have the right to exploit and enslave black people and control these and many other natural products of Africa.

Alfa-alfa grass	Diamonds	Phosphates
Animal fats	Fish	Peaches
Animal hides	Flax	Pears
Animal oils	Fruits	Parsnips
Alluminum	Gold	Persimons
Agate	Glass sand	Poultry
All-spice	Ground nuts	Precious stones
Blue diamonds	Grapes	Querry stones
Barley	Grain flour	Quinces
Blue stone	Graphite	Raisins
Brass	Hemp	Rice
Borax	Hogs	Rubber
Bread fruit	Herbs	Stock
Barks	Incense	Silica
Birds	Iron ore	Swamp grass
Bananas	Juices	Silver
Bristle grass	Kola nuts	She butter
Beads	Lime	She butter oil
Cement	Lead	Sesame
Cocoa	Lodestone	Sugar cane
Citron	Millet	Sugar beets
Cotton	Milk	Sheep
Cocoanuts	Minerals	Sponges
Cocoa butter	Maple syrup	Soda
Copra Kernels	Mineral oil	Soap stone
Castor oil beans	Manganese	Slate
Corn	May apples	Spices
Coffee	Mineral rock	Salts
Cattle	Mineral wool	Soy beans
Cloves	Molasses	Sea weeds
Cork	Onyx	Teak wood
Cipra	Oranges	Tin
Copper	Okra	Tobacco
Crude oil	Pulps	Vegetables
Coal	Palm oil	Vegetable oil
Chalk	Platinum	White diamonds
Carbon	Prunes	Whet rock
Clays	Pepper	Wild animals
Dates	Pearls	Wool
		Zinc — etc, etc,

When these plundering, self-styled christian nations stop trying to fool the justice of God, they will automatically stop bleeding and fooling themselves, then justice and peace will come to this war weary world.

"BROOKS FIELD"

Private Robert H. Brooks was killed in action near Fort Stotsenburg, P. I. December 8th, 1941.

He was the first casualty of the armoured forces in the second world war. The parade ground at Fort Knox Kentucky was named in his honor.

This soldier was serving in a so-called white outfit that never suspected he was a Negro.

His untimely and heroic death revealed the fact that his fine parents; were highly respected Negroes living quietly in the jim-crow state of Kentucky.

⟶∿⟵

* MRS. ANNA ELEANOR ROOSEVELT *

Mrs. Anna Eleanor Roosevelt, wife of President Franklin D. Roosevelt, has been proudly photographed in Negro groups more often than the wives of all other American Presidents combined.

CORTEZ W. PETERS

Mr. Cortez W. Peters, Worlds Typewriter Champion, can type at the sparkling speed of 130 words a minute and at the same time talk on an entirely different subject.

Cortez W. Peters Business Schools are located in Washington, D. C., Baltimore, Md. and Chicago, Ill. His graduates are working all over the world — 1944.

⟶∿⟵

DR. CHARLES R. DREW AND BLOOD BANKS
1942

Dr. Charles R. Drew was born in Washington, D. C. about 37 years ago. He is one of the worlds great medical technicians, and has served for a number of years on the staff of Howard University. He has graduated from a number of colleges in America and abroad. He is an all around athelete, and knows more about blood seperation, blood refrigeration, and blood preservation than any other doctor of his day.

Dr. Drew was selected in 1940 by the Board of Medical Control, of Blood Transfusion Betterment Association of New York, as medical supervisor of the Blood Plasma Division, in charge of the collecting of blood for the British army. And from his technical knowledge thru the Red Cross, blood banks for civilians and soldiers have been set up thruout the world.

This modest highly trained Negro has published more than fifteen scholarly papers on blood transfusion and blood banks. The historian who writes the march of medicine cannot omit the name of Dr. Charles R. Drew, who established a great technical institution that has refused in many ways to cooperate with the race that produced the genius who established the institution.

DR. WALTER F. JERRICK

Dr. Jerrick was born March 2, 1894, in British Guiana came to America when a boy, worked his way through Lincoln University, won a scholarship to European schools; studied in London and Scotland. His Philadelphia, Pa office is crowded with ailing people who know the difference in his diagnosis, the magnificance of his medicine and the hospitality of his handshake.

1940 U. S. CENSUS OF NEGROES BY STATES

Not Including the Thousands of Passable Negroes

North Dakota	201	Indiana	121,916
Vermont	384	California	124,306
New Hamshire	414	Oklahoma	163,849
South Dakota	474	District Of Columbia	187,266
Wyoming	556	Michigan	208,345
Idaho	595	Kentucky	214,021
Nevada	664	New Jersy	226,973
Montana	1,120	Missouri	244,386
Utah	1,235	Maryland	301,931
Maine	1,304	Ohio	339,461
New Mexico	4,672	Illinois	387,446
Oregon	2,565	Pennsylvania	470,172
Washington	7,424	Arkansas	482,578
Minnesota	9,928	Tennessee	508,736
Rhode Island	11,024	Florida	514,198
Wisconsin	12,158	New York	571,221
Colorado	12,176	Virginia	661,449
Nebraska	14,171	South Carolina	814,164
Arizona	14,991	Louisiana	849,303
Iowa	16,694	Texas	924,391
Connectticut	32,992	North Carolina	981,298
Deleware	35,876	Alabama	983,290
Massachusetts	55,391	Mississippi	1,075,578
Kansas	65,138	Georgia	1,084,927
West Virginia	117,754	Total	12,865,518

FORTUNE IN CHURCHES

1940 Census Value of Church edifices reported by 34,-250 Negro Churches amounted to $126, 531,551. which represents 4.8 per cent of all the value of all reported edifices in America.

FOOLISH FUNERALS

I dedicate this article to the few Morticians and Ministers who are advising poor people to carry Negro Insurance and avoid a large debt after death, which usually follows foolish flamboyant funerals.

Our lodges can do more marching, the relatives can do more regretting, the motor cars can do more back-firing, and the officiating minister can say more to an unreplying corpse than any race on earth.

A Negro who is well known and is a member of two or three organizations is more respected after his death, than he has ever been during his life.

In some localities it takes three days and three nights to cry over the corpse of a colored man that we long have cursed.

It takes all day to bury the remains of a lodge man with his dues paid up, or a popular gambler with his morals run down.

While venerable old men, orphan children, and mistreated Mothers are often forgotten and thrown in an unmarked grave in potters field without fern or flower, minister or mourner, without sympathy or ceremony, and without Bible or benediction.

At Negro funerals you can see more costly unpaid for caskets, hear more lengthy obituaries, and finally see more empty epitaphs than you have ever seen before.

One can never tell about the wealth or worth of the deceased by the cost of the casket, for some small two inch Negroes have large two mile funerals.

We are christians and beleive that after death we shall meet again, to know each other in a land where we shall be free and faultless, holy and happy.

But the way we weep at funerals and cringe at cremation, one would think that we were infidels, believing that death ends all, instead of christians that believe in the ressurection into an everlasting life.

81

American Presidents have been interned with services that lasted less than an hour, but when a Negro is buried, the cemetery must stay open for the race that likes to be late.

Parades must be held, prayers must be said, papers and telegrams must be read, the congregation must see the corpse, and the minister who should be merciful will not stop preaching until emotion is shouting, and sympathy is weeping, and relatives are all heart sick from the sermon of sorrow.

The more funerals white people have the more money they put in the bank, the more funerals we have the more we go in debt.

Ignorance never carries much life insurance, but it wants plenty of pomp from a ten cent policy.

One would think that money rained from the skies the way we foolishly bury it under the ground.

When our relatives die instead of giving them a decent burial in a near-by well-kept cemetery, we go in debt and waste the insurance money to take the corpse way back down south to some mud-hole near Mississippi.

No special cemetery will erase the sin or save the soul, and when the day of judgement comes God can find your grave whether you are buried in Boston or Birmingham.

If we believe in another life after death, we should also know that a cheerful smile is the finest flower ever seen at a funeral.

And death seems less terrible when we discard the black and wear raiments of white and garments of grey.

A cheerful smile on the face of a friend at a funeral is a better indication of christain faith than the crepe on the arm, and tear on the cheek.

THE TRUTH ABOUT AFRICA

Africa is like any other country, it goes to those who can take it, and stays with those who can keep it.

Altruistic Africa, a great Fatherland, forgotten and unwanted by its mistreated children.

Africa, where civilized nations send missionaries and muskets, Bibles and battleships, mandates and marines, Kings to hold natives down and cannons to blow them up.

Africa, where millionairies send missionaries from lynch loving America to lie on the Lord, graft on God, harp on heaven, cheapen the church and peddle their sour soulless jim-crow religion to the natives in the jaws of the jungles.

Africa, where white men exhibit, exploit, exaggerate, experiment and excruciate.

Africa, the garden of genius and generosity, where nature gives equality and quantity without quarrel or question.

Africa, the birth place of hospitality, where smiles first began to wreath the cheerful cheeks of chastity.

Africa, the home of Ham and the neighborhood of Nimrod, the land of song and summer.

Africa, where Nordics go to get rich, and Negroes shun in order to stay poor.

Africa, exploited by Firestone, fundamentalist, foreigners, freelancers, fakirs, and fogies.

Africa, where robbers get rubber, prospectors get pearls, gamblers get gold, capitalist get concessions, militarists get Morroco, and Africans get almost nothing.

Africa, raped and robbed by those who get rich, forsaken and forgotten by those who stay poor.

Africa, the land of faith and fortitude, scenery and sience, patience and providence; the father of fashion and the mother of music.

Africa, the black man's country, full of white faiths, white faces, white men's flags, white men's Bibles and white men's bayonets.

Africa, where the natives have been exploited by manufacturers in time of peace and killed by marksmen in time of war.

Africa, where English aviators rain liquid fire on natives who kneel with prayerful hands outstretched to heaven.

Africa, with fig and flower, moss and magnificence, vine and veriegation, cocoanut and climate, scenery and season.

Africa, with diamonds and deserts, Africa with pearls and possibilities, Africa, with minerals and modulations, Africa, with ivory and incense, Africa, with warmth and welcome, Africa with game and glory.

Africa, the embryo of revolution, the vineyard of veracity, the cradle of creation.

Africa, where daimonds are set in diction, pearls are wrought in pathos, and ebony is woven in eloquence.

Africa, God's country, fought for by Nordics and forgotten by Negroes. There will never be peace on earth as long as black people are enslaved on the continent of Africa.

=⟐=

YOU ARE THE MAJORITY GROUP

You are now living in ONE WORLD. Regardless of what you are called locally you are part of the colored races of this one world. You are over EIGHTY PER CENT of the worlds population. You are not the minority group. You are the MAJORITY GROUP. The Caucasians are a MINORITY GROUP with a majority complex. And you are really the MAJORITY GROUP with a MINORITY COMPLEX. And out of that distorted state of mind comes that dreadful INFERIORITY COMPLEX.

BESSIE COLEMAN

If your imagination is good you can fancy a dauntless brownskin Larybird, using her aeroplane for a fountain pen, the exhaust of smoke for ink, and God's blue sky for her paper.

That's brave little Bessie Coleman writing her name across the sky in a sensational aerial act of spectacular penmanship.

She was blessed with the power of perseverance, and walked many long miles each day to learn, and teach her people how to fly. She was fearless as Franklin, as noble as Newton, as brave as Bruno, and as wonderful as Wright.

She knew that tireless wings were faster than tender feet. She loved the music of the motor and the purr of the propeller; she disputed with the Eagle and broke his brilliant record.

She believed in service rather than sentiments, she loved performance better than pleasure, she gave exhibitions and not excuses. She pushed her silver wings thru the clefts of the lazy clouds and brought back a wonderful story of the stars.

She flew over the Royal Palace, encircled Eifel Tower, and spanned the English Channel.

The whole world was her country, she flew all flags and examined all facts, and learned that people are pitiful when they have no power.

She performed while her people prayed, she dared while they danced, she soared while they slept.

She asked Negro business men to pool their funds and help to motorize the sky. She received no reply, and was forced to consider others who took an interest in her cause.

She had a vision and saw great airships crossing Seas and bombing helpless humanity; she fought and flew ahead of her time and was greatly misunderstood.

She knew the poverty of the past, the possibilities of the present, and the forces of the future.

She knew a bird was faster than a buggy, that winging was better than walking, and that aviation was greater than ignorance.

The most scientific of her sex, the most courageous of her color, the most progressive of her people.

If she had a fault it was in the lack of fear.—not in her doing, nor daring.

She liked distance and laughed at danger; she was a patient pioneer that loved adventure and knew the price of progress.

She was thrilling thousands at Jacksonville when the fatal crash came. The gears jammed, something went wrong and brave Bessie Coleman was hurled to instant death.

People who could have promoted her program while she lived, wept and worshiped her after she died.

I saw the machine from which she fell; twisted wires; burnt metal and broken wheels. I thought of the countries she crossed, I thought of the thousands she thrilled, and I thought of the price she paid for being a vigilant veteran and teaching the scheme of the sky.

Brave little Bessie Coleman fought with a stout heart and died beneath broken wings; she tried to awaken her people, then reported back to God and wore her purple plume to heaven.

WATCHING MY RACE GO BY

The old type Negro has no library and wants no liberty, he is never preparing but always parading; he borrows from his neighbors to bet on the numbers. He has no thirst for thought, but likes plenty of thunder, he thinks more of chitterlings than he does of children, he neglects his brains for his bunions. He is always complaining about his complexion, he is a soldier in a war and a slacker in a riot. He hates science and loves superstitions, he talks about luck, but won't listen to logic. He is concerned about dying but not about living, he resides in Minnesota as well as Mississippi.

He is the loud-talking, tatteling, tough type of Negro, and for his kind, we need a few thousand funerals.

A new intellectual Negro is rising like a marble shaft in the gray dawn of determination.

It took the Caucasian race several centuries to produce Washington and Webster, Whitlock, Whitney and Whitman, Watt and Wells, Watterson, Wadsworth, Westinghouse and Willkie.

Emmerson and Edison, Stone and Steimetze, Eckner and Armstrong, Arkwright, Einstein and Ingersoll, Shakespeare and Shelley, Lock and LaPlace, Ford and Fisk, Fulton and Foraker, Darwin and Darrow, Debs and Dickens, Franklin and Phillips, Lovejoy and Longfellow, Lincoln, Logan, and Lindberg.

Brown and Bacon, Bell and Beecher, Bismarck and Bessemer, Bruno and Blackstone, Burk, Brisbane and Burbank.

Newton and Knox, Wright and Roosevelt, Roentgen and Rosenwald, Rockne and Ruth, Revere, Redpath and Riley.

Voltaire and Volney, Stalin, Sumners and Sousa, Colt and Caruso, Henry, Hitler and Haeckel, Holmes and Harvey, Pullman and Paderewski, Pitt and Paine, Gladstone, Garrison and Galileo, Moody, Milton and Michael Angelo.

Marconi and Magellan, Perry and Plato, Guttenberg and Goldsmith, Tobey and Tolstoy, Talmadge and Thompson, Keats and Kepler, Conkling and Corbett, Kant, Copernicus, Columbus and Keller.

When the conquering Caucasian had three thousand years of training behind him, the chattel slave still had three hundred years of bondage before him. But now the colored man is persuing the pages of his own performance.

The race loving Negro visits the graves of Young and Europe, he is proud of men like Pushkin, Pickens and Pollard; and he follows the achievements of Flipper and Flowers. He thinks of Walcott and Woods, Ellington and Washington, Williams and Woodson.

He muses with Overton and L'Overture, Louis, Alexander and Abbott, Walker and Wheatley, Whitney and Whipper. He reads about Banneker and Batson, Bethune and Butler, Braithwaite and Burroughs. And he knows Redmond, Revels and Randolph. His library has the works of Truth, Tubman and Turner. And he dreams about Groves and Gans, Garvey and Gandhi, Grant, Gaines and Gilpin. He laughs with Alonzo and Attucks, Allen, Armstrong and Austin. He admires Cook and Coleman, Carver and Cullen. He remembers Dumas and Davis, Douglass and Dett, DuSable, DuBois and Dunbar. He sings with Hayes and Henson, Jackson and Johnson. He travels with Scott and Scarborough, Sissle and Simmons.

He is proud of Thompson and Trotter, Tanner and Taylor. He communes with McCoy and Miller, Malone and Montgomery, and he knows the history of Harrison, Hamilton, Hunter, Yergan, Vessey and Vernon.

He sits on the front porch of the future, applauding the pagant of progress, while watching my royal race go by.

THOMAS FULLER

Alexandria, Va., is almost within sight of the United States Capitol. However, a woman of that city by the name of Mrs. Elizabeth Cox owned a fourteen year old black slave by the name of THOMAS FULLER.

The records in this case as in the case of many slaves, is rather meager. Dates and many details have either been lost or purposely destroyed. It is known, however, that THOMAS FULLER was stolen from his home in AFRICA and brought to America in chains along with hundreds of other exploited slaves.

THOMAS FULLER was a prodigy, though he could neither read nor write. But he perfected a high-speed scientific system of mental enumeration that puzzled the academic world.

He could rapidly give the number of years, months, weeks, days, hours, minutes, and seconds in any given period of time a person chose to mention.

Allowing in his calculations for all the leap years that occured within that space of time.

He could also give the number of miles, rods, yards, feet, and inches in any given distance. Even the diameter of the earths orbit.

He seldom made a mistake, and could accurately do in a few seconds what so-called experts could only do in many hours with their pencils.

This versatile Virginian calculator attracted the attention of such great men as Dr. Benjamin Rush of Philadelphia, Pa., and many other noted scientists of his day.

Any one was free to interrupt him in the process of his mental calculations, and engage him on any other subject. But he was neither hampered, nor distracted.

He would start in where he left off, and could give any, and all, of the phases, and stages through which his faultless flying figures had passed.

THOMAS FULLER was once asked how many seconds a man of eighty years, some odd months, weeks, days, hours, and minutes had lived. He gave the exact number in one minute and a half.

The man who questioned him took his pen, and in several hours he figured it out. Then he told TOM that he must be wrong, because the figures he gave were too great. Then TOM said to the questioner, your figures would be right but you left out leap years. The white man figured again, and found TOM'S figures were correct.

THOMAS FULLER the able African calculator died in slavery when about eighty years of age. He was perhaps the greatest arithmetician that the world has ever known.

His color would have barred him from membership in the Royal Society of London, or the Academy of Science in Paris, or the Technical Engineers of America.

However, Einstein could have been his servant, Newton could have been his pupil, and Euclid could not have been his teacher.

God is not prejudice, wisdom knows no race, and genius caters to no color.

Page 22 Edward Johnson's History of the Negro Race in America 1894.

STEVEN LANDRUM

For many years Uncle Steve Landrum as he was affectionately called, was a well known figure around Glasgow and Louisville, Kentucky.

He did not know the year of his birth. He was the child of slave parents, and might have been a slave himself.

However, at the time of his death in Kentucky, August 30th, 1923, he was perhaps around 85 or 90 years of age.

He had never attended any kind of a school, and could neither read nor write.

Despite his illiteracy he was one of the country's best business men.

He could figure things out in his head long before an expert could do the job with adding machine, or pencil and paper.

Steve Landrum was a very exact, polite, and positive man. He could add substract and multiply with the highest degree of accuracy.

He kept no books but carried his figures and findings in his Hamitic head.

He worked hard, and made the money he possessed, and was known to be worth at least one hundred thousand dollars. He made a business buying and selling real estate, and collecting his rents.

He never loaned money and did not care much for banks. And he was hard on people who tried to cheat or be dishonest.

He never had a lawsuit, and was very industrious, thrifty, tolerant, and sober.

He made no exhibit of prosperity, even when his income was over five hundred dollars per month.

When his tax expert asked him questions about his yearly income and expenses, he could without hesitation tell him the exact amount, the hundreds of dollars and even the pennies that he took in, and payed out during the year.

He could figure up the net income down to a cent, before the tax expert could get his pencil and paper ready.

Perhaps no other living man had such a calculative mind as Uncle Steve Landrum.

Once he sold a business house for nine thousand dollars, he received the money in cash and divided it among his relatives, with the understanding that each one would buy a home.

He carried thousands of dollars to and from his home, and to the bank in an old half gallon tin bucket, and in an old fashion split basket.

Once he received an ordinary friendly letter from his Niece in Louisville, telling him of her children having colds, because of the leaky roof in the old house in which she lived. He immediately got in touch with his Attorney, E. H. Smith and had him buy her a three thousand dollar home. That home was immediately deeded to his Niece.

Before his death he bought each of his relatives a home. He also bought land and had a two story school house built for the Colored children of the neighborhood.

He wore old ragged faded clothing. And often had hundreds of dollars in the pockets and patches of his unpressed garments.

In his will he provided for his relatives, and also for the support of a Normal school for Negro youth.

He would not live in a fine house, and neither would he purchase an automobile.

He requested that at his death, his body should be buried in a cheap casket, and that he be given a modest funeral.

Uncle Steve Landrum embraced an altruistic religion that always kept him happy, by doing for other people, the things that they were unable to do for themselves.

RACE NEWSPAPERS AND PERIODICALS

ATLANTA DAILY WORLD, Atlanta, Ga.
ADVANCE THE, Portland, Ore.
AFRO-AMERICAN THE, Presbyterian, Charlotte, N. C.
ALABAMA TRIBUNE, Montgomery, Ala.
ARKANSAS SURVEY JOURNAL, Little Rock, Ark.
ASHVILLE RECORD, Ashville, N. C.
BALTIMORE AFRO-AMERICAN, Baltimore, Md.
BUFFALO CRITERION THE, Buffalo, N. Y.
BLACK DISPATCH THE, Oklahoma City, Okla.
BUFFALO STAR THE, Buffalo, N. Y.
BOSTON CHRONICLE THE, Boston, Mass.
CLEVELAND CALL AND POST, Cleveland, Ohio.
CALIFORNIA EAGLE THE, Los Angeles, Cal.
CAROLINA TRIBUNE THE, Raleigh, N. C.
CHICAGO BEE, THE, Chicago, Ill.
CLEVELAND GAZETTE, THE, Cleveland, Ohio.
CHARLESTON MESSENGER, Charleseton, S. C.
CHICAGO WORLD, THE, Chicago, Ill.
CHRISTIAN REVIEW, Philadelphia, Pa.
CHARLOTTE POST, Charlotte, N. C.
CHICAGO DEFENDER, THE, Chicago, Ill.
COLORED CITIZEN, THE, Pensacola, Fla.
CRISIS, THE, New York City.
DAYTON FORUM, Dayton, Ohio.
DETROIT TRIBUNE, Detroit, Mich.
DALLAS EXPRESS, THE, Dallas, Texas.
EAST TENNESSEE NEWS, Knoxville, Tenn.
EAST WACO NEWS, Waco, Texas.
FLASHLIGHT HERALD, Knoxville, Tenn.
GARY AMERICAN, Gary, Ind.
GUARIDIAN, THE, Boston, Mass.
GUIDE. THE. Omaha. Neb.
HOUSTON DEFENDER, Houston, Texas.
INDIANAPOLIS RECORDER, Indianapolis, Ind.
INFORMER, THE, Houston, Texas.
IOWA BYSTANDER, Des Moines, Iowa.

JOURNAL OF NEGRO HISTORY, Washington, D. C.
KENTUCKY REPORTER, THE, Louisville, Ky.
KANSAS CITY CALL, Kansas City, Mo.
LOUISIANA WEEKLY, New Orleans, La.
MUSKOGEE LANTERN, Muskogee, Okla.
MOBILE ADVOCATE, Mobile, Ala.
NEW YORK AGE, New York City.
NORFOLK JOURNAL AND GUIDE, Norfolk, Va.
NASHVILLE GLOBE, Nashville, Tenn.
NEW YORK AMSTERDAM NEWS, New York City.
NORTHWEST ENTERPRISE, Seattle, Wash.
OMAHA GUIDE, Omaha, Neb.
OPPORTUNITY, New York City.
PHOENIX TRIBUNE, Phoenix, Arizona.
PHILADELPHIA TRIBUNE, Philadelphia, Pa.
PALMETTO LEADER, Columbia, S. C.
PHILADELPHIA INDEPENDENT, Philadelphia, Pa.
RICHMOND PLANET, Richmond, Va.
PITTSBURGH COURIER, Pittsburgh, Pa.
SAVANNAH JOURNAL, Savannah, Ga.
SAN DIEGO INFORMER, San Diego, Cal.
SAINT LOUIS AMERICAN, St. Louis, Mo.
SAINT LOUIS ARGUS, St. Louis, Mo.
STAR OF ZION, Charlotte, N. C.
SHREVEPORT SUN, Shreveport, La.
VOICE OF NEGRO BUSINESS, Detroit, Mich.
VOICE PEOPLES, New York City.
WHOLE TRUTH, THE, Memphis, Tenn.
WACO MESSENGER, Waco, Texas.
WISCONSIN ENTERPRISE, Milwaukee, Wis.
WASHINGTON TRIBUNE, Washington, D. C.
WORLD, THE, New Bern, N. C.

INTER-RACIAL MARRIAGE LAWS
IN THE UNITED STATES

At the present time there are 48 States in the Union. 30 of these States forbid marriages between whites and Negroes. In these 30 States white men may, and do have children by Negro women with immunity.

In many of these 30 States bawdy houses with Negro girls who are only allowed to cater to white men are running wide open.

In many of these 30 States the Negro girl who is raped or wronged by a white man, has no standing in the local courts, and can find no law to compel the white man to care for his illegitimate half-white child.

Listed below are 18 States that permit inter-racial marriages between Caucasians and men and women of African descent. Thus, giving some hope of protection to the woman of color.

1943

CONNETTICUT	NEW JERSY
KANSAS	MAINE
IOWA	NEW HAMSHIRE
VERMONT	RHODE ISLAND
OHIO	MASSACHUSETTS
MICHIGAN	ILLINOIS
PENNSYLVANIA	WISCONSIN
NEW MEXICO	MINNESOTA
NEW YORK	WASHINGTON

SOME OF OUR
PROMINENT INSURANCE COMPANIES

Afro-American Life Insurance Co., Jacksonville, Fla.
Atlanta Life Insurance Co., Atlanta, Ga.
Central Life Insurance Co., Tampa, Fla.
Domestic Life & Accident Insurance Co., Louisville, Ky.
Dunbar Mutual Insurance Society, Cleveland, Ohio
Excelsior Life Insurance Co., Dallas, Texas
Federal Life Insurance Co., Washington, D. C.
Fireside Mutual Insurance Co., Columbus, Ohio
Great Lakes Mutual Life Insurance Co., Detroit, Mich.
Golden State Mutual Life Insurance Co., Los Angeles, Cal.
Good Citizen's Mutual Benefit Assn., New Orleans, La.
Guaranty Life Insurance Co., Savannah, Ga.
Keystone Life Insurance Co., New Orleans, La.
Louisiana Industrial Life Insurance Co., New Orleans, La.
Mammoth Life and Accident Insurance Co., Louisville, Ky.
North Carolina Mutual Life Insurance Co., Durham, N. C.
Peoples Insurance Co., Mobile, Ala.
People's Industrial Life Insurance Co., New Orleans, La.
Pilgrim Health & Life Insurance Co., Augustus, Ga.
Protective Industrial Insurance Co., Birmingham, Ala.
Provident Home Industrial Mutual Life Ins. Co., Philadelphia, Pa.
Richmond Beneficial Insurance Co., Richmond, Va.
Safety Industrial Life, & Sick Benefit Assn., New Orleans, La,
Southern Life Insurance Co., Baltimore, Md.
Southern Aid Society Of Virginia, Inc., Richmond, Va.
Standard Industrial Life Insurance Co., New Orleans, La.
Supreme Camp Of the American Woodman, Denver, Col.
Supreme Liberty Life Insurance Co., Chicago, Ill.
Union Protective Assurance Co., Memphis, Tenn.
United Mutual Benefit Association, New York City
Universal Life Insurance Co., Memphis, Tenn.
Victory Industrial Life Insurance Co., New Orleans, La.
Victory Mutual Life Insurance Co., Chicago, Ill.
Virginia Mutual Benefit Life Insurance Co., Richmond, Va.
Winston Mutual Life Insurance Co., Winston Salem, N. C.
Western Union Mutual Insurance Co., Detroit, Mich.

THE SEVEN FAMOUS MEMBERS
OF THE 44TH CONGRESS

This Congress had more Negro Members than any other Congress.

JOSEPH H. RAINEY, South Carolina.
ROBERT SMOLLS, South Carolina.
BLANCHE K. BRUCE, Mississippi, U. S. Senator
MAJOR J. R. YLNCH, Mississippi.
JEREMIAH HARALSON, Alabama.
JOHN A. HYMAN, North Carolina.
JOSIAH T. WALLS, Florida.

Some Of The Colored Races Througout The World
British Empire Colored Races At The Outbreak Of The Second World War

British India	300,000,000	Aden (Protectorate and the Islands of	
British Malaya	5.237,841	Perim)	48,338
British N. Borneo	270,233	Socotra	12,000
Brunei	30,135	Maldive Islands	79,000
Sarawak	442,900	Samaliland	
Hong Kong and Territories	1,028,619	Protectorate	344,700
South West		British W. Indies	2,880,087
Africa (M)	292,401	British Honduras	57,767
British S. Africa	3,845,006	British Guiana	337,521
British E. Africa	14,061,506	Falkland Islands	
Zanzibar		and S. Georgia	3,908
Protectorate	235,428	Territory of	
British W. Africa	27,453,432	Papua	300,000
Anglo Egyptian		New Guinea (M)	666,000
Soudan	6,342,477	West Samoa	59,306
Ceylon	5,312,548	Pacific Islands	426,127
	Total	368,924,280	

Native Population Of French West African Colonies Before Second World War

Dahomey	1,078,638	Ivory Coast	1,811,392
Guinia	2,217,799	Mauretania	321,679
French Soudan	2,773,730	Niger	1,473,509
Haute-Volta	3,039,093	Sengal	1,529,474
	Total	14,245,814	

Other African Colonies—Colored Population Before Second World War

Belgium Congo	20,,000,000	Italian Samoliland	650,000
Italian Eretrea	403,582	Italian Tripoli	1,000,000
	Total	22,053,582	

CELEBRATED NEGROES WHO ARE SAID TO HAVE MARRIED WHITE WOMEN

FREDRICK DOUGLASS — Abolitionist, Orator and Statesman.

ROBERT PURVIS—Anti-slavery Orator.

JOHN F. QUARELS—Friend of Charles Sumner.

PROF. W. S. SCARBOROUGH — Howard University, Prof of Languages.

JOSEPH ANTONIO MACEO—Son of a great Cuban General.

PHIL EDWARDS—Celebrated athelete of British Guiana.

HERBERT NEWTON—Versatile song writer.

EUGENE NELSON—Wealthy Physician

JEROME PETERSON—Medical Student, Columbia Univ.

DR. THOMAS W. PATRICK—Harvard graduate.

GEORGE R. WILLIAMS—Called the "dwarf turtle boy"

WILLIAM S. STEWART—Garage owner New York City.

JACK JOHNSON—Former Heavyweight Champion of the world.

JULIAN STEELE—Married Mary DAWES. Said to be a relative of Vice President Charles Dawes.

HENRY O. TANNER—Internationally famous Artist.

GEORGE W. SCHUYLER — Celebrated writer, his daughter "PHILLIPA" is the greatest musical genius of the age.

(J. A. Rogers, SEX AND RACE, Vol. II, Page 236)

RICHARD WRIGHT—Author of "Native Son"

RIO OTTLEY—Author of "New World A Coming".

SUCCESSFULLY PASSING FOR WHITE

This writer knows of a white woman clerk in a large high class down town Pittsburgh department store who hates the very sight of Negroes, and avoids serving them whenever possible.

She would likely drop dead if she knew that her beloved husband with whom she sleeps every night is actually a light skinned mulatto Negro.

FAMOUS WHITE PEOPLE WHO ALLEGEDLY HAD NEGRO BLOOD IN THEIR VEINS

HANNIBAL HAMLIN—Civil War Vice President.
DANIEL WEBSTER—Great American Statesman.
ANDREW JACKSON—7th President of the United States.
GEORGE W. FAIRFAX—Cousin of Lord Fairfax.
SIR WILLIAM PHIPS—First Royal Governor of Massachusetts.
CATESBY COCKE—U. S. Senator from Virginia.
HENRY TIMROD—Celebrated Civil War Poet.
MRS. FRANK LESLIE—Refined and cultured writer.
COMMODORE O. H. PERRY—Hero, battle of Lake Erie.
WARREN G. HARDING—Late President of the United States.
ADA ISAACS MENKEN—Actor, Poetess, Dancer.
VINCENT KINGSEY HULL—Head of a great steamship company.

(J. A. Rogers, SEX AND RACE, Vol. II, Page 249)

NOTED WHITE MEN WHO ALLEGEDLY MARRIED COLORED WOMEN

ABRAHAM—Married a black woman—Gen. 25:I.
MOSES—The great law giver, married a black woman. 1st. Cor. 2:3.
CLARENCE KING—Eminent Geologist and Engineer.
JAMES BANKS—Wealthy Harvard Graduate.
EMIL E. UMLAUFF—Highly respected Chief of Police, Phoebus, Va.
J. E. MASON—Wealthy west coast business man.
ARTHUR W. FROST—Wealthy sugar planter.
JOSEPH M. PERKIS—New York City aristocrat.
LEONARD KIP RHEINLANDER—Wealthy member of the N. Y. 400.
ITALIAN COUNT—Married Josephine Baker, celebrated Negro singer.

(J. A. Rogers, SEX AND RACE, Vol. II, Page 228)

LEN ZINBERG—Noted Writer.
VINCENT R. B. VANNECK — London millionaire, married Victoria O. Thomas, Negro actress. Reception in London's famous Savoy Hotel.

(Pittsburgh Courier, August 14, 1943)

FAMOUS WHITE MEN WHO ARE CREDITED WITH HAVING HAD NEGRO MISTRESSES

BENJAMIN FRANKLIN—Great American Statesman and Inventor.

THOMAS JEFFERSON—Great Statesman and Patriot

PATRICK HENRY—Statesman and lover of liberty.

COLONEL RICHARD M. JONES—9th U. S. Vice Pres.

SOSTHENE ALLAIN—Wealthy native of Louisiana.

MAJOR PINCHBACK—Of Louisiana.

JEFFERSON DAVIS—Head of the Southern Confederacy

HENRY CLAY—Celebrated orator of Kentucky.

JOHN TYLER—10th President of the United States.

ZACHARY TAYLOR—President of the United States.

COLONEL THOMAS H. BENTON—U. S. Senator from Mississippi.

MAJOR MARCUS B. WINCHESTER — Mayor of Memphis.

DAVID DICKSON—Agricultural Scientist, Georgia.

A. T. MORGAN—Member Mississippi Legislature

G. THORNTON—North Carolina Politician, 1866. He lived among Negroes and was buried from a Negro church.

LAFCADIO HERN—Noted American Writer.

THADDEUS STEVENS—Reconstruction Orator. (Robert Ripley says, he requested, and was buried in a Negro cemetary).

(J. A. Rogers, SEX AND RACE. Vol. II, Page 221)

PEARL BUCK in
"PEARL BUCK SPEAKS FOR DEMOCRACY"
Foreword by MRS. FRANKLIN D. ROOSEVELT
Page 3

With all the evils that Hitlerism has, at least it has one virtue, that it makes no pretense of loving its fellow-man and wanting all people to be free and equal.

Everybody knows where nazism stands and what to expect of it. Cruel as it is and dangerous as it is to civilization, it is less cruel, and it may be less dangerous in the end, than the sort of democracy which is not real enough or strong enough to practice what it preaches.

MRS. FRANKLIN D. ROOSEVELT Foreword—
"PEARL BUCK SPEAKS FOR DEMOCRACY"

The colored American thanks to an education in democracy, now really wants to see his country a democracy. When he defends the United States of America he does not want to do so segregated and limited.

This contradicts his idea of democracy. He has grown up a good deal since the world war, and he has not forgotten that war.

He is willing to fight and die again, but not for something he does not possess anyway.

THE MEANING OF AMERICA

"Courtesy Chicago Daily News"—ANP

Died January 5th, 1943, Tuskegee, Ala.

Highlights In Life Of The 'Wizard Of Tuskegee'

From slave to world renown scientist who was bought for the price of a horse to become a benefactor of mankind and "God-Angel" of the South—that epitomizes the career of Dr. George Washington Carver, a gentle man of keen intellect, shy disposition, indefatigable energy, unfailing patience and a christian to the core.

Dr. Carver has been honored by Presidents of the United States, European royalty, scientific societies, educational institutions at home and abroad, the Congress of the United States, great industrial geniuses, religious bodies, the members of his race and topped by his crowning achievement in being recognized by the people of dixie as the one man who saved the economy of the south and gave it industrial independence.

Notable highlights in the life of America's best known agricultural-scientist follows:

Elected member of Iowa State College faculty, 1894.

Teacher and director of agricultural research, Tuskegee Institute, since 1896.

Elected member of Royal Society of Arts, London, 1917.

Awarded Spingarn Medal, 1923.

Honorary degree, Simpson College, Iowa, 1928.

Collaborator, Bureau of Plant Industry, U.S. Department of Agriculture, 1935.

Recipient of Roosevelt Medal, 1939.

Creator of 160 products from the peanut.

Discovered over a 100 products from the sweet potato.

Made 60 articles of value from the pecan.

Extracted dyes from southern clay.

Honored by the American Chemical Society.

Life story featured in the movies by Metro-Goldwyn-Mayer.

Citizens contributed bronze bust to Tuskegee Institute.

Establishment of the Carver Creative Research Laboratories at Tuskegee.

Appeared before the Congressional Ways and Means Committee.

Honorary member, Mark Twain Society of New York.

Named "Man of the Year" by the Progressive Farmer, farm journal, 1942.

Gave Henry Ford, motor magnate, formula for synthetic rubber.

Gave camouflage paint formula to U.S. Army.

Developed cheap paint formula.

Gave medical profession formula to treat infantile paralysis.

Recipe for making delectable dishes from wild weeds.

Recipient of the first annual award of the Catholic Committee of the South.

Humanitarian Award of the Variety Clubs of America, 1940.

Headlined, second Freedom's People radio series sponsored by the U.S. Office of Education.

National Honor Roll on the Wall of Fame, World's Fair, 1939-41.

Schomburg Collection Honor Roll.

Honored by the following universities and colleges: Duke University, New York University, Yale University, Furman University, University of N. Carolina, Greensboro · College for Women, Howard University, Washington College, Mississippi State College for Women and Millspas College, Mississippi.

"Courtesy Pittsburgh Courier"

MRS. FRANKLIN D. ROOSEVELT ANSWERS A QUESTION

Page 25 "LADIES HOME JOURNAL" July, 1942

Negro soldiers guard the railroad bridge in our Maine town. Recently I invited one of the soldiers to dine with us and our whole family (white) is being criticized. Should I have done this?

I see no reason why you should not have invited a Negro soldier to dine with you if you wished to do so. I imagine there are some white people whom you would not like to have in your home, and there might be Negroes whom you would not like to have there either. Just because a person is black, there is no reason why you should not be kind to him if he is a nice person.

After all, we have got to face the fact that we have allies today in India and in China, and that our attitude toward the other races of the world must become one of co-operation rather than one of domination, if we are going to lay a basis for a better world in the future. I believe, of course, that the emphasis in our relationship with the Negroes should be to see that they get their full rights as citizens, but the personal equation is one which every person has to decide for himself. We are free to act as our own conscience and our own inclination dictate. We live in a free country where we are not forced to do anything about our personal relationships which we do not feel like doing.

—ELEANOR ROOSEVELT.

UNCLE STEVE LANDRUM
With His Basket Full of Money

J. A. ROGERS
Historian, Lecturer, Thinker,
and World Traveler.

MARIAN ANDERSON
Celebrated Contralto Singer

JESSE OWENS
World's Festest Runner

SOJOURNER TRUTH
Great Abolitionist Spokesman

COL. JOHN C. ROBINSON
Great Air Ace in Ethiopian-
Italian War.

ISAAC MURPHY
Three Times Winner of Kentucky Derby,
Greatest Jockey of All Time.

Schmeling out on the ropes

JOE LOUIS
Knocking Out Max Schmeling, June 23rd, 1938

CLAUDE HARVARD—Georgia
Inventor of Automatic Gauging and Sorting
Machine for Ford V-8 Piston Pins.

BENJAMIN BANNEKER—Maryland
Inventor of First Clock to Strike
the Hour.

NORBERT RILLIEUX—New Orleans, La.
Inventor of Evaporating Pan for
Refining Sugar.

ELIJAH McCOY—Michigan
Inventor of Lubricating Oil Cup for
Machinery.

JACK JOHNSON
Knocking Out James J. Jeffries, 15 Rounds
Reno, Nevada, July 4th, 1910

GRANTVILLE T. WOODS—Ohio
Inventor of Electrical Air brakes, Incubator
and Other Electrical Devices.

JAN E. METZELIGER—Massachusetts
Inventor of Machine for
Lasting Shoes.

ANDREW J. BEARD—Alabama
Inventor of Automatic Car-coupling Device,
Known as the "Jennie Coupler."

ROBERT A. PELHAM—Michigan
Inventor of Pasting Machine and Tabulating
Device in the Matter of Compiling Statistics.

VITAMINS, PROTEINS AND CALORIES

In Chattel Slavery the Southern Masters ate the white bread, and the best looking foods, and gave the black slave what he considered the coarsest victuals and the worst grub on the plantation.

So the poor slave ate the bran bread, whole-wheat bread, corn pone, rye-bread, oat-meal, johnnie-cakes, and the unwanted products of barley, spinach, mush, greens, corn on the cob, cabbage and black eyed peas. He also ate pigs feet, hog ears, salt pork, hog head, hog head cheese, liver, lights, cracklings and crackling bread, neck bones, back bones, chitterlings and ox tail soup.

The master did not know that those unwanted foods contained many of the Vitamins, Proteins, and Calories from which these skilled women kitchen magicians, and architects of appetite would mould and make generations of world-record-breaking champions.

With well seasoned non-fancy foods, earnest prayers, and the will to win, our enslaved fore-parents have produced thousands of celebrated Negroes who have paradoxically made their mark in every worthy walk of life.

By mixing versality with our Vitamins, perservance with our Proteins, and courage with our Calories, we have been able to do less with more and more with less than any other race on earth.

— REV. ROSS D. BROWN.